RUSSIA UKRAINE, PUTIN ZELENSKYY

YOUR ESSENTIAL UNCENSORED GUIDE TO THE RUSSIA - UKRAINE HISTORY AND WAR

VALENTINE GREEN

CONTENTS

INTRODUCTION

Since the first three months of 2022, the conflict between Russia and Ukraine has captured the attention of the whole world. Ever since rumors began that the Russian military was preparing to troop en masse to the border of Ukraine and invade the neighboring country, news outlets have featured the ongoing military campaign and covered the crisis round-the-clock. The reports have been consumed by viewers from all corners of the globe, an obvious sudden interest in one of the most significant conflicts of recent times.

The global community was just emerging from the effects of the COVID-19 pandemic, and everywhere countries were either slowly reopening their economies and removing various restrictions, or grappling with the fresh surge of recent variants of the virus while attempting to return to some semblance of normal. The world was hoping for a respite from the harrowing and exhausting two years brought about by the pandemic, but as the conflict between Russia and Ukraine escalated, it became apparent that this would be the next big hurdle for the global community to deal with.

The effects of the unfolding crisis in this part of the world soon reverberated around the globe. Oil prices surged, financial markets were shaken, large multinational corporations pulled out of Russia, and many nations soon announced a barrage of economic sanctions on Russian President Vladimir Putin and his family as well as numerous other top officials and oligarchs from his country. The humanitarian crisis also brought the escalating problem right to the doorsteps of neighboring countries as millions of refugees from Ukraine streamed across the border, trying to escape the ongoing bombardment and danger at home.

Soon, talks of an even bigger global war were floating around in 24-hour cable news channels, podcasts, online communities, and on social media. As the United Nations and NATO began to call for Russia to cease its invasion of Ukraine, all eyes were on China, a known ally of Russia. As lines of demarcation began to be clearer and much of the global community resonated in condemnation of Russia's actions, China adopted a more neutral position. For now, it appears that China is sticking to this stance, but many pundits have cautioned that if China gets involved in the conflict in one way or another, the situation could deteriorate very quickly.

Europe, for the most part, has banded together and provided logistical support and other forms of aid to Ukraine, although these countries have steered clear of directly sending troops to help Ukrainian forces fighting off Russian invaders. Other Western countries such as the United States and Canada have also sent significant material and financial aid to Ukraine. And in another interesting turn of events, the images of Ukrainian President Volodymyr Zelenskyy leading Ukrainian fighters and putting his life at risk by being in the front lines have captivated people around the world, even encouraging a number of volunteer fighters from different countries to travel to Ukraine and offer to fight alongside Ukrainian forces and civilians who are already staving off the Russian troops.

It would be interesting to note that, up until the events of the past few months, many people around the world did not know much about the country of Ukraine, beyond the usual historical backgrounds and associations with Russia and the post-Soviet era. Apart from the common depictions of Ukraine and its citizens in popular culture, particularly in films, television series, and books, many people know very little about Ukrainians or their nation. But because of the focus of mass media over the last few months, and as global audiences are exposed to the gallant stand that Ukrainians have put up defending their country from invaders, the world now has a better understanding of this country and its citizens.

What has been happening in Ukraine in the first part of 2022 is the culmination of a long-standing conflict between the two countries that dates back to 2014, and in the next few chapters, you will get a historical perspective of how Russia and Ukraine reached this boiling point. What was the reason behind the disagreements between the two countries, and what escalated the issues and caused the Russo-Ukrainian War that all of us are now monitoring?

In order to really understand the root of these events, one has to understand the historical and cultural background of this region of the world. Indeed, Russia and Ukraine have a shared history that goes back many decades, and the similarities and comparisons between their cultures cannot be ignored or simply dismissed. What becomes apparent as one analyzes the histories of these two nations, however, is how the fight for democracy and the yearning for freedom and justice became the difference for Ukraine, and these are the very ideals that are now being threatened due to the relentless military offensive being undertaken by Russia.

Truly, what is happening at the moment in Ukraine is a crisis that will have lasting and far-reaching effects throughout the modern world. No matter how near or far you may be from the center of the ongoing war, you should be knowledgeable of the events and have an understanding that goes beyond just what is being shared on social media or the news outlets. It should be the comprehension that as citizens of the world, we are all connected to each other in more ways than we are often aware, and we should be prepared to stand up for what we believe in when challenged by forces that seek to undermine the human need for liberty, truth, and happiness.

CHAPTER 1

THE HISTORICAL RELATIONSHIP BETWEEN RUSSIA AND UKRAINE

Russia and Ukraine are embroiled in an ongoing conflict that has dominated the world stage in 2022, and when one takes a closer look at the extensive and intertwined history of these two neighbors, a better understanding of the issues between the two states can be achieved. Their shared history dates back almost one thousand years, when Kyiv, which is now the capital of Ukraine, was the epicenter of the very first Slavic state, Kyivan Rus. This state was the birthplace of modern-day Russia and Ukraine.

Their common heritage can also be seen in the religious parallels that have always been similar between the two states. In A.D. 988, the grand prince of Kyiv and pagan prince of Novgorod, Vladimir I, converted to the Orthodox Christian religion. The prince was baptized into the Christian faith in the city of Chersonesus in Crimea. This conversion unified the populations, although conflicts did crop up occasionally throughout the centuries.

Ukraine, in particular, is no stranger to turbulent times caused by various neighboring states encroaching into its territory or realigning its borders. In the 13th century, Mongol invaders from the east conquered Kyivan Rus and ruled over this region for some time. Then in the 16th century, invaders from Poland and Lithuania also came in from the west and staked their own claim to part of Ukrainian territory. When war broke out between the Polish-Lithuanian Commonwealth and the Russian Tsardom in the 17th century, many areas situated east of the Dnieper River in Ukraine fell under the control of imperial Russia and became known as the "Left Bank." Meanwhile, those on the "Right Bank" or west of the Dnieper River remained under Polish control until 1793, when this region was annexed by the Russian Empire.

The 20th century brought much transformation to this part of the world, starting with the communist revolution of 1917. The Russian Revolution became known as one of the most significant and politically important events of the century as it brought an end to the centuries-old Russian Imperial power and the Romanov dynasty. During this violent upheaval, leftist revolutionary leader Vladimir Lenin led the Bolsheviks of Russia to seize control of the country, overthrowing the rule of the czar. Over time, this faction of the Bolsheviks would become a more organized group—the Communist Party of the Soviet Union.

There were actually two revolutions that rocked Russia and eventually ushered in the era of the Soviet Union. Conditions in the country were ripe for the social unrest of that year, as decades of poverty and underdevelopment plagued Russia. In the early 1900s, Russia was viewed by most of Western Europe as a backwards country, and it was one of the poorest nations in the region, overrun by peasants and poor workers. There were food shortages due to the rapid population boom and a number of expensive wars.

Because of the difficult conditions, widespread protests were carried out by Russian industrial workers against the monarchy in 1905. That year, the Bloody Sunday massacre occurred, where the Russian czar's troops attacked hundreds of unarmed protesters, many of whom were critically wounded or killed.

This angered more workers throughout Russia and set off the 1905 Russian revolution, with workers going on strike all around the country and putting a stop to its economy. After this internal conflict, Czar Nicholas II promised widespread reform with the establishment of Dumas, or representative assemblies that were focused on making changes to the system.

Then, World War I erupted, and in August of 1914 Russia found itself embroiled in the fight between the Serbs, French, and British allies on one side, and Germany on the other. The war became another costly mistake for Russia, which was already weak economically. Russian casualties during World War I were the most of any nation, mainly because the Germans were just too strong and advanced in comparison. Russia suffered from rising inflation, food and fuel shortages, and other disruptions to its economy.

Czar Nicholas left St. Petersburg, the capital, and led the Russian Army front during World War I. In his place, his wife Czarina Alexandra and her advisor Grigory Rasputin, took over the reins of the government, and their numerous blunders and unpopular decisions angered the Russian population even further. This led to the March 8th, 1917 revolution where huge crowds of protesters marched in St. Petersburg (then known as Petrograd) and began to clash with army garrison troops. After several days of violent demonstrations, Czar Nicholas agreed to abdicate the throne, and a provisional government took over.

This provisional government, helmed by up-and-coming Russian lawyer Alexander Kerensky, was founded in opposition to violent social reform, and was focused on implementing equality, freedom of speech, and giving labor unions the liberty to protest. Kerensky also continued the unpopular Russian participation in World War I, and this caused food and supply shortages to worsen. Crime and violence became commonplace throughout the country as desperate citizens tried to fend for themselves amidst the declining conditions.

Then, in the latter part of 2017, the Bolshevik Party, headed by Vladimir Lenin, initiated their bloodless takeover of the provisional government. Leftist revolutionary groups took over various government buildings and strategic outposts throughout the capital of Petrograd and installed a new communist government headed by Lenin. This became the first communist state of the world, with Lenin as its dictator/ruler.

Civil war broke out soon after this coup, with Russian forces divided into the Red Army, which was loyal to the Bolshevik faction headed by Lenin, and the White Army bankrolled by democratic socialists, capitalists, monarchists, and other allied supporters. The Russian Civil War dragged on for about six long years, exacerbated by several events such as the Bolshevik faction's execution of the Romanovs on July 16th, 1918. In 1923, the Red Army declared they had won the Civil War, and the Soviet Union was established.

When the Soviet Union was founded, Ukraine was one of several countries that became a part of this large communist region, along with Belarus, Armenia, Estonia, Azerbaijan, Georgia, Latvia, Kyrgyzstan, Kazakhstan, Moldova, Lithuania, Tajikistan, Uzbekistan, Turkmenistan, and Russia. This conglomeration became officially known as the United Socialist Soviet Republic. As the very first Marxist-Communist state in the world, it became a way for Communist ideology to spread rapidly to other countries. The Soviet Union was, at the time, one of the largest and most powerful nations, and it occupied almost one-sixth of the total land area of Earth.

The Communist Party, headed by Vladimir Lenin, led the formation of the USSR. After the death of Lenin, the revolutionary leader from Georgia, Joseph Stalin, took over and started a dictatorial rule that was brutal and feared, yet it spurred the Soviet Union to superpower status both in terms of economy and military might. Stalin was the leader until 1953, and during his reign, he implemented a number of Five-Year

4

Plans that emphasized economic growth, industrialization, military build-up, and arms production.

Stalin also strictly enforced the collectivization of the agricultural sector of the member republics of the USSR. Peasants in rural areas were mandated to take part in collective farms, with their livestock or land taken away from them. Higher-income farmers were arrested and executed, and the state confiscated their properties. The Communists did this with the belief that the consolidation of individual farms into state-controlled collective farms would ramp up their agricultural productivity, but in fact, the collectivization proved to be disastrous.

Many citizens resisted the collectivization push in the countryside, and overall agricultural productivity fell sharply. The decrease led to massive food shortages across the Soviet Union, and a Great Famine persisted from 1932-1933. This famine was particularly devastating for Ukraine, where the famine was known as the Holodomor, which meant *starvation* and *the infliction of death*. It is estimated that about 13 percent of the total Ukrainian population, or 3.9 million people, died during the Ukrainian famine.

The decimation of the population became such a big problem that Stalin needed to relocate large numbers of Russians and other Soviet citizens to repopulate Ukraine, particularly in the eastern regions. The vast majority of these imported populations did not speak Ukrainian and had no ties to the region at all, and this repopulation effort would be a key factor in many later conflicts leading to the issues today. The eastern part of Ukraine had stronger ties to Russia and tended to support leaders who leaned toward Russia in their policies, while Western Ukraine had more affinity with the Austro-Hungarian Empire, as well as Poland. As such, the western part of the country backed Western-leaning politicians.

The divide also became more apparent when it came to culture and customs. Those in the eastern part of Ukraine spoke more Russian and were generally Orthodox in their religion, while those in the West spoke Ukrainian and were mostly Catholic. In later years, and even when Ukraine became an independent state, unity within the country became an arduous task because of this divide that started with the repopulation after the famine years.

It was not just the famine, however, that citizens of Ukraine and the entire Soviet Union had to endure under the brutal reign of Stalin. Through his secret police, he eliminated his political opponents and silenced dissidents, especially during the Great Purge between 1936 and 1938. During this time, millions of Soviet citizens were deported, imprisoned in forced labor camps called Gulags, or tortured. About 600,000 Soviet citizens were executed during this period.

When World War II erupted, the Soviet Union found itself in an unlikely and uncomfortable alliance with Great Britain and the United States, with Nazi Germany and Japan on the opposing side. When the war ended, the alliance soon dissipated, especially as the Soviet Union began to set up communist-leaning governments in those Eastern European countries that it had helped to liberate from the Nazis. The British and the Americans became concerned that this would spread communist ideology further to Western Europe and the rest of the world, and they began to take steps to halt this.

In 1949, the United States, Canada, and their allies in Europe formed the North Atlantic Treaty Organization or NATO, and this alliance sent a strong message to the USSR-led alliance. In response, the Warsaw Pact was consolidated by the Soviet Union and its Eastern European allies in 1955. This period became known as the Cold War, infamous for instances of heightened tension, economic maneuevers, and propaganda campaigns between both sides. The Cold War would continue until the eventual collapse of the Soviet Union in 1991.

One particularly tense part of the Cold War was the Cuban Missile Crisis, which happened under the leadership of Nikita Khrushchev, the successor of Stalin. Khrushchev was less repressive to Soviet citizens compared to Stalin, and in fact he released many political prisoners, shut down the notorious Gulags/labor camps, removed a lot of the restrictions on art and freedom of expression, and strived to raise living conditions. But in 1962, the Soviet leader decided to install nuclear weapons from an outpost in Cuba which was just 90 miles from the coast of Florida. This set off the Cuban Missile Crisis, and set the region on the precipice of war.

The crisis soon dissipated without any real conflict, much to the relief of the world. But within the Soviet Union, the damage to Khrushchev's leadership was far-reaching. Mounting dissatisfaction with his rule was exacerbated by the worsening relations between the Soviet Union and China, as well as the continuing problems of food supply shortages across the USSR. Eventually, influential members of the Communist Party instigated his removal from office in 1964.

The last leader of the Soviet Union was Mikhail Gorbachev. He assumed power in 1985, amid a struggling Soviet economy and a political system that was in chaos. Gorbachev sought to address these problems and keep the Soviet Union intact through a series of concerted reform policies. The first one, the *glasnost* (Russian for openness) plan, aimed for political openness, more liberty for citizens, a push toward a freer press, and opening the elections to other parties aside from just the Communist Party.

Gorbachev's other plan, the *perestroika* (Russian for restructuring), focused on doing just that, restructuring the badly-hit Soviet economy by adopting a hybrid communist-capitalist system that was similar to China's. Under this system, the Politburo, or the policy control wing of the Communist Party, still had the reins of the economy's direction, but market forces and trends would be allowed by the state in order to influence much of the production and development decisions. The reform policies of Gorbachev were well-meaning, but the results took a lot of time to really make an impact. At the same time, the increased freedom made many of the Soviet citizens braver in calling for independence, particularly in the Eastern European republics.

When a political revolution swept through Poland in 1989, other peaceful movements spread across Eastern Europe. By the end of the year, the USSR was in clear crisis, and the tide of independence could no longer be contained. The crisis was worsened by an unsuccessful coup attempt made by loyalists from the Communist Party in August 1991. Democratic factions, under the leadership of Boris Yeltsin, continued to call for independence and turned popular opinion further against Gorbachev.

On December 25th, 1991, Gorbachev finally stepped down as the leader of the USSR. By December 31st, 1991, the Soviet Union was officially dissolved. For Ukraine, this meant a newfound status as an independent nation, but the transition was far from simple for the republic. Long used to the principles of communism, the introduction of capitalism and democratic processes was messy for the country's population. Also, the differences between the eastern and western parts of Ukraine became even more apparent post-independence, especially as many Ukrainians from the east viewed Russian rule as more stable and familiar.

In Donetsk, Luhansk, and much of the eastern parts of Ukraine, many of the citizens are descendants of the Russian peasants and immigrants who were sent there during Stalin's regime to repopulate the country. They see themselves as more connected to their Russian legacy, and it has been harder to bring the country together because of this divide. According to Adrian Karatnycky, a former fellow at the Atlantic Council of the United States and an expert on Ukraine, "The biggest divide after all these factors is between those who view the Russian imperial and Soviet rule more sympathetically versus those who see them as a tragedy."

Recent political events in Ukraine continue to reflect this general fault line between the various regions of the country and how the citizens are sympathetic to Russia and the former Soviet rule. During Ukrainian presidential elections of 2004 and 2010, for instance, the voting trends were, by and large, still consistent with how populations tended to support Western- or Russian-leaning candidates. Also, during the Orange Revolution of 2004, much of Kyiv and Western Ukraine called for greater integration and cooperation with Europe, pushing back against calls to align the country more with its Russian neighbor.

In many ways, relations between Russia and Ukraine after the fall of the USSR has been heavily influenced by the Kremlin's intention to still exert influence over the former Soviet republics, even though the union has been officially dissolved. To Russia, its influence over its "near abroad" is its own way to limit the expansion of NATO's power into the Eastern bloc, so Russia has always tried to do what it can to keep its influence alive in Ukraine and other states.

A primary example of this would be the occupation and eventual annexation of Crimea by Russia in 2014. The events started to unfold when separatists in the eastern Ukrainian region of Donbas, who were loyal to Russian rule, initiated an uprising which led to the installation of the People's Republics of Luhansk and Donetsk. The movement was mostly backed by Russia, and as the conflict escalated, it gave Moscow a justification to step in and annex Crimea, despite widespread condemnation by the world. Russia also staged a referendum in the Crimean peninsula which purportedly sought the citizens' consensus on whether to reunite with Russia. Reunification was reportedly supported by 97 percent of voters, although no election observers from outside countries were present during the vote. To this day, the referendum has not been recognized internationally.

Relations between Russia and Ukraine have been contentious since the collapse of the Soviet Union, but more so in recent years. The uprising in the Donbas region, for instance, continues until this day, with around 14,000 people already killed. Although the two sides managed to avoid widespread military conflict for some years, the region was still in constant tension. Several agreements sought to maintain some semblance of peace in the region, but the stalemate continued, even through the election of current Ukrainian President Volodymyr Zelenskyy in 2019.

It is interesting to note how Russia positions itself when it comes to Ukrainian affairs. At times, it presents itself as simply a neutral observer or a mediator, as in the case of the establishment of the People's Republics of Luhansk and Donetsk. Although evidence has pointed to Russia's consistent backing of these separatist uprisings, Russia continues to assert that it has no hand in the independence movements whatsoever. On the other hand, Russia does flex its military muscle when it deems necessary, as in the occupation of Crimea. And with the escalation of conflicts in recent weeks and the unrelenting attacks on Ukraine, it has become clear to all that Russia has set its eyes on further carving out a bigger chunk of Ukrainian territory.

The various historical conflicts between Russia and Ukraine need a deeper understanding in order for anyone to really see how things reached a boiling point and escalated in 2022. In the next chapter, you will read all about the more intricate details of these conflicts between the two nations and delve into the complicated relationship that eventually deteriorated into the disastrous war playing out on the world stage today.

CHAPTER 2

THE BACKGROUND OF THE RUSSO-UKRAINIAN WAR

The troubled relationship between Russia and Ukraine reflects many decades of intense actions and reactions, and it remains to be seen whether there will be any real solutions in the foreseeable future. Even when Ukraine lost its fight for independence in the early 20th century and was absorbed into the Soviet Union, the region never fully integrated with the rest of the Russian framework, and pushed to maintain its own language and culture.

Adding to the not-so-favorable view of Russia among many Ukrainians is the many atrocities that their homeland endured while under Soviet rule. Most notably, the Great Famine of the 1930s, when vast swaths of Ukrainian farmlands were forcibly taken by Soviet authorities. Wheat and other crops were confiscated, and the ensuing famine resulted in the deaths of almost four million Ukrainians.

When Ukraine declared itself to be an independent state after the collapse of the Soviet Union in 1991, it moved closer to Western Europe and democratic allies. However, because the eastern part of the country is populated by a substantial number of descendants of Russian immigrants, cultural ties with Russia have remained deep, and in a number of instances these ties have caused flare-ups that have led to larger conflicts, as in the case of the Ukrainian Revolution of Dignity in 2013-2014.

Also known as the Euromaidan Revolution, this point of Ukrainian history is still the subject of much controversy. During this revolution, thousands of Ukrainian protesters called for the ousting of then-President Viktor Yanukovych, largely seen as a Russia-leaning leader. During his four-year tenure, Yanukovych and his cronies were accused of stealing almost $100 billion from the country's coffers, a substantial amount given that Ukraine's economy at the time was equal to that of the state of Nebraska.

Aside from corruption, his pro-Russia policies also angered many Ukrainians and caused the revolt. In particular, Yanukovych announced that Ukraine was abandoning the Association Agreement with the European Union, which was the basis for closer economic cooperation between Ukraine and the EU, and he manuevered to align the country with the Russian counterpart instead. The abandonment of the Association Agreement was supported by Vladimir Putin.

This was the last straw for a big part of the Ukrainian population, and protesters streamed into the Maidan square in Kyiv, Ukraine's capital, to call for Yanukovych to vacate his post. In retaliation, the embattled president commanded police forces to shoot any protesters who were opposing his rule. However, instead of scaring off the protesters, this further emboldened the citizens, and the crowds continued to grow bigger with each passing day. Finally, when it became clear that he could no longer contain the movement, Yanukovych escaped to Russia, vacating his post. This was the first major victory of the Ukrainian Revolution of Dignity.

The victory was not without huge cost for the people of Ukraine. There were bloody confrontations between police officers and protesters, with deaths and injuries reported on both sides. Hundreds of protesters were imprisoned, but eventually they were released in February of 2014 as part of an amnesty deal. The European Union threatened to impose sanctions on Ukraine if the government failed to de-escalate the worsening violence, and many of those economic sanctions were eventually implemented. The already struggling economy of Ukraine was damaged even further because of the political crisis and the sanctions from the European Union, and it would take some time for the country to regain its footing even after the ousting of Yanukovych.

An interim Ukrainian government was established with Arseniy Yatsenyuk, a Fatherland leader, as the prime minister. Presidential elections were announced for May 2014. During this time, the conflict began to boil over to the eastern portion of Ukraine as pro-Russian demonstrators refused to back down. In Crimea, several groups of armed men in uniforms with no identifying marks as to which side of the conflict they belonged started to occupy government buildings and surround airports in Sevastopol and Simferopol. They overran the parliament building in Crimea and hoisted a Russian flag, denounced the newly-installed Ukrainian government, and declared a separate prime minister for Crimea—Sergey Aksyonov, head of the Russian Unity Party.

The crisis in Crimea deepened further as Moscow admitted that they had sent Russian troops to the region to maintain peace and order. Voice and data communication between Crimea and Ukraine were cut off, and Ukrainian acting president Oleksandr Turchynov condemned this as a violation of the sovereignty of Ukraine. Meanwhile, Putin justified the actions of Russia as necessary in order to safeguard Russian citizens and military assets in the Crimean region.

Even among Ukrainians who were loyal to the government and resisted Russian influence, the attitudes toward the effects of the Revolution of Dignity were mixed, especially after a few years. For instance, in 2014, about 15 percent of the Ukrainian population lived below the poverty line, but in 2019 it increased to a quarter of the population. After the revolution, the Ukrainian economy experienced a recession and a devaluation of its currency, caused by the various conflicts that began to take place and the severing of economic ties with Russia, which was Ukraine's major market for many of its food exports and industries related to manufacturing, aerospace, and military equipment.

Putin also claimed that many of the ethnic Russians living in the eastern regions do not support the pro-Western government of Ukraine, an assertion which is not entirely unfounded. This assertion also emboldened Russia to support a referendum in Crimea on whether the region will secede from Ukraine and become a part of the Russian Federation. First, the Crimean parliament voted for secession from Ukraine on March 6th, 2014, and then a public referendum was scheduled for March 16th of the same year. According to the Crimean parliament, 97 percent of the public voted in favor of separating from Ukraine and joining Russia. The result was congratulated by Russia, but further soured the situation between Russia and Ukraine.

Western countries refused to recognize the referendum, citing reports of irregularities and harassment throughout the voting process and polling locations. Ukraine's interim government also refused to accept the result of the referendum, and Yatsenyuk was resolute in the position that Crimea remain part of Ukraine. Soon after, the EU and the United States imposed various sanctions on Russian officials as well as key members of the parliament of Crimea, including the freezing of assets and travel bans. By March 18th, just two days after the referendum, Putin was already in a meeting with Aksyonov and several other representatives, and they signed a treaty which officially made Crimea a part of the Russian Federation, despite mounting criticism from Western countries.

Skirmishes between both sides soon followed. A few hours after the treaty was signed, masked gunmen attacked a Ukrainian military base located just outside Simferopol, and a Ukrainian soldier was killed. Russian troops started to take over various military bases in the Crimean peninsula, among them the naval headquarters of Ukraine located in Sevastopol. Ukraine's interim government ordered the immediate evacuation of around 25,000 military personnel along with their families out of Crimea. On March 21st, as the annexation treaty was ratified by the Russian parliament, Putin formally signed the law making Crimea a part of Russia.

In the midst of the dispute, Yatsenyuk had another critical issue to address: the economy of Ukraine. He negotiated with the International Monetary Fund (IMF) and fleshed out a bailout package intended to resolve the $35 billion worth of unpaid financial obligations of the country. He also travelled to Brussels, Belgium to meet with EU officials, and on March 21st he signed a segment of the association agreement with the EU that Yanukovych refused to sign back in November of 2013. Soon after, the IMF came out with an $18 billion loan proposal to assist Ukraine, with certain conditions that needed to be met, such as austerity measures, devaluation of the hryvnya currency, and cutbacks on state-sponsored subsidies that were designed to keep natural gas prices lower for consumers.

Russia ramped up pressure in order to maintain its control over Crimea, including ending a 2010 treaty extending its lease on the Sevastopol port in exchange for substantial discounts on the price of natural gas. With the abrogation of the treaty, the cost of Russian-supplied natural gas in Ukraine shot up by around 80 percent within weeks. Russia was upfront regarding its continued economic maneuvers against the interim government of Ukraine, but was less forthcoming regarding its other plans to extend its reach into Ukrainian territory. But in April 2014, NATO announced that it had discovered the presence of over 40,000 Russian troops along the Ukrainian border, seemingly poised for military action at any time.

Clashes continued consistently throughout the region as pro-Russian militias with powerful weapons attacked various government buildings in the eastern part of Ukraine, particularly in the cities of Luhansk, Donetsk, Kramatorsk, and Horlivka. Gun battles became commonplace between loyalist forces of Ukraine and pro-Russian gunmen touting Russian arms and unmarked uniforms. In response, Turchynov offered a surrender deadline for pro-Russian forces who had taken over government buildings, offering them immunity from prosecution in exchange for surrendering. Kyiv threatened to step up military action if the separatists did not surrender, but the deadline passed and no incidents took place, as Turchynov appealed to the United Nations to step in and send peacekeepers to Ukraine's eastern region in an attempt to regain control.

Turchynov did try to de-escalate the situation further by indicating his approval of one of the major demands of the pro-Russian separatists, which was a referendum on whether to convert Ukraine into a federation and granting greater autonomy at the regional level. This was meant to keep the Ukrainian state intact while also appeasing the desire of pro-Russian factions to have less oversight and control over their affairs. This was followed by an emergency meeting in Geneva attended by representatives from Ukraine, Russia, the European Union, and the United States.

The Geneva parties unanimously agreed to take steps to resolve the ongoing conflict in Ukraine's eastern region, but this turned out to be mostly lip service on the part of Russia as it continued to position its military along the border with Ukraine. Also, pro-Russian forces continued to take over more government buildings and set up armed checkpoints in major thoroughfares in the peninsula. There were high-profile incidents of abduction and detention of many Western and Ukrainian journalists, Ukrainian police officers and security service members, and even eight members of a monitoring mission conducted by the Organization for Security and Cooperation in Europe (OSCE).

More sanctions were announced by the United States and the European Union to pressure Russia to cease its actions, but the sanctions had very little effect on Russia's campaign to retain control of annexed Crimea. The government of Ukraine restarted its push back against the pro-Russian camp in Slov'yansk on May 2nd. That same day, the conflict reached the city of Odessa, a part of Ukraine that had been able to avoid skirmishes. Dozens of pro-Russian protesters were killed when the building they were staying in was engulfed in a fiery blaze.

Putin made a personal trip to Crimea on May 9th, 2014, the Victory Day holiday commemorating the defeat of Nazi Germany during World War II. A few days before the Putin visit to Crimea, an advisory body known as the Council for Civil Society and Human Rights published its report on the independence referendum that was held in Crimea back on March 16. The report countered much of Moscow's assertions regarding the referendum; the Council said the voter turnout was only between 30 to 50 percent, and a little over half of the voters had voted to become part of Russia. This coincided with two self-declared separatist governments in Donetsk and Luhansk also preparing to hold their own independence referenda amidst bloody clashes between both camps.

The referenda were held on May 11th in those two cities, but once again, the results were not recognized by Ukraine or the West. There were numerous reports of masked gunmen in polling centers, widespread instances of voters casting multiple ballots, and even the seizure of 100,000 "yes" votes by Ukrainian police who intercepted the ballots from separatists in Solv'yansk. The results of the independence referendum favored annexation by Russia, to which Putin responded by saying that the voters' will must be respected. The EU announced additional sanctions against Russian interests in protest of the widely-discredited referenda.

As fighting continued in Eastern Ukraine, the rest of the country was also focused on the presidential elections held on May 25th, 2014. Voter turnout was particularly strong in spite of disruptions in some areas, particularly in Donetsk and Luhansk where polling stations were occupied by pro-Russian militia and ballot boxes were forcibly taken. Petro Poroshenko, a Ukrainian billionaire, claimed victory with more than the 50 percent required to win the election outright in the first round. After the election, fighting intensified in the eastern section of the country, but this did not hinder Poroshenko from being sworn into power on June 7th.

Poroshenko was intent on somehow restoring peace in the separatist-controlled eastern regions of Ukraine, and he offered a number of proposals in an attempt to work with the pro-Russia separatists. But the conflicts continued unabated, and evidence of Russian interference continued to mount as more arms and equipment were seen in the frontlines. In particular, three Soviet-era fighter tanks showed up in a number of Ukrainian towns close to the border with Russia. Loyal forces were able to recapture the city of Mariupol on June 14th, but not without suffering a significant loss of life when pro-Russian forces shot down a transport plane with 49 citizens aboard.

Still, Poroshenko continued to call for a ceasefire, and even offered amnesty to separatist groups who would surrender. He also sought the help of former president Kuchma to meet with the rebel groups and attempt negotiations. For his part, Putin also appeared to want to de-escalate the conflict in Eastern Ukraine, and he walked back on his previous authorization of Russian troops entering Ukrainian territory. These attempts did little, however, to turn the tide of fighting on the ground, especially after the association agreement was signed with the EU on June 27th, further aligning Ukraine with the West.

Loyal Ukrainian forces were able to take back Kramatorsk and Slov'yansk in the following weeks, and government forces were able to make more inroads against the rebels, despite the use of more sophisticated weapons and equipment purportedly from Russia. The pro-Russian forces, in particular, enhanced their air defense capabilities and were able to shoot down a Ukrainian transport plane and a Ukrainian fighter jet. However, both attacks were alleged by Ukrainian military officials to be the work of Russian military forces themselves, citing evidence that the separatist militias did not have the capabilities to shoot down planes from longer range.

Things took a turn for the worse on July 17th, 2014 when Malaysia Airlines Flight 17 was shot down as it flew over the Donetsk region of Ukraine. The passenger plane was carrying 298 people on board, and had taken off from Amsterdam Airport Schiphol en route to Kuala Lumpur, Malaysia. The Boeing 777-200 had a crew of 15 and 283 listed passengers with about ten different nationalities represented. Majority of the passengers on board the ill-fated passenger plane were from the Netherlands (193 passengers).

Flight 17's flight plan was over the entire span of Ukraine, including the eastern region where loyalists and separatists were actively fighting. Three days prior to the incident, Ukrainian aviation authorities had set a minimum altitude restriction of 10,000 meters or 33,000 feet for aircraft flying through Eastern Ukraine; this was after a Ukrainian military transport jet was blown out of the sky. At the time that the Malaysian passenger jet was shot down, there were three other passenger planes in the same radar control area. The cabin crew maintained routine communication with air traffic controllers in the vicinity, and then disappeared from radar screens.

Because of the ongoing conflict in the region, the investigation took longer and encountered a number of complications, but researchers were able to rule out pilot error, mechanical failure, inclement weather, or any onboard mishaps such as fire or explosions. Instead, the evidence pointed to the crash being the direct consequence of the detonation of a warhead from a radar-guided Buk missile, which was a surface-to-air missile system that could reach even the cruising altitude that Flight 17 was in. The missile detonated several feet away from the cockpit, and did not hit the aircraft directly, but the explosion sent hundreds of fragments of shrapnel through the plane's fuselage.

Because of the explosion, the cabin crew died instantly as the front section of the plane broke off. The jet's wings, passenger compartment, and tail remained in mid-air for about one more minute, then separated and hurtled to the ground. Wreckage from Flight 17 was scattered over a 50-square-kilometer area (20 square miles), with most of the wreckage focused in farmlands southwest of Hrabove, a mostly separatist-controlled territory of Ukraine.

The crash sent shockwaves all over the world, and was particularly devastating for Malaysia Airlines as the company was still reeling from the disappearance of another one of its passenger aircraft, Flight 370, just a few months prior to the downing of Flight 17. The Ukrainian government was quick to point the blame on pro-Russian forces, and presented intercepted audio recordings of separatist forces discussing having shot down a plane minutes after the crash. But the separatists and their Russian supporters denied responsibility for the crash and had their own explanations. When a United Nations resolution seeking to establish a tribunal for investigating and assigning culpability for the incident was presented, Russia vetoed the move.

Later, video evidence showed rebel forces sifting through the wreckage of Flight 17 shortly after the crash and expressing dismay or surprise that it was a civilian aircraft, not a military jet. Then, in September of 2016, the Dutch-commissioned prosecutorial team officially presented evidence that the missile had been fired from a separatist-controlled territory in Ukraine with the use of a weapons system from Russia. The weapons system apparently was returned to Russia on the very same day. On June 19th, 2019, charges were filed against three Russians and one Ukrainian in connection with the crash of Flight 17, with the primary suspect being Igor Girkin, a former colonel of the Russian Federal Security Service or FSB.

Because of the crash, international attention on the fighting in Ukraine increased. Forces loyal to Kyiv were able to advance gradually and recapture rebel-held strongholds such as Luhansk and Donetsk. Russia continued to maintain that it did not have any direct involvement in the military conflict, but Moscow did acknowledge in August of 2014 that a number of Russian paratroopers had been captured within Ukrainian territory. A ceasefire agreement on September 5th between Russia and Ukraine, signed in Minsk, Belarus, managed to slow down the conflict, although skirmishes did not completely stop.

Poroshenko then introduced a wave of economic and political reforms in preparation for Ukraine's application for EU membership by 2020; his proposals were approved by voters during the parliamentary elections on October 26th, 2014. But just several days later, pro-Russian separatists in Luhansk and Donetsk conducted local elections in direct violation of the ceasefire agreement signed in Minsk. This flared up conflict between the two sides once more, and heavy fighting as well as the presence of Russian military equipment once again exacerbated the situation.

A major turning point seemed to have been reached on February 12th, 2015, when a 12-point peace plan was proposed by leaders from Russia, Ukraine, Germany, and France. The peace plan detailed several conditions, including the immediate cessation of fighting between both sides, the withdrawal of heavy weapons and equipment, the release of prisoners being held on both sides, and the withdrawal of foreign troops that were currently within Ukrainian borders. By the first few days of September 2015, heavy weapons were pulled back by both loyalists and separatists, and the peace agreement seemed to hold for the most part, despite sporadic violations of the truce.

Within the next few years after the truce, the eastern region of Ukraine became relatively quiet, while the attention of the Ukrainian population shifted to the economic and political reforms promised by the administration of Poroshenko. However, allegations of corruption and economic failures hounded his time in office, and in the presidential election of March 2019, television actor and political newcomer Volodymyr Zelenskyy was able to capture the imagination—and the votes — of the Ukrainian populace.

Zelenskyy garnered over 30 percent of the vote during the first round of polling, against the 16 percent taken by Poroshenko. The second round of polling on April 21st concluded with Zelenskyy winning by a landslide, with 73 percent of the total votes. From the get-go, Zelenskyy vowed that his primary goal as president of Ukraine was to establish lasting peace in the country's war-ravaged eastern region. Zelenskyy's Servant of the People party also captured an absolute parliamentary majority in the legislative elections.

One of Zelenskyy's first moves as leader of the country was to set forth a peace settlement calling for both loyal Ukrainian forces and Russian-supported separatists to leave the "contact line" in East Ukraine, where many conflicts often took place. Majority of Ukrainians, already tired from years of war, supported the settlement, despite critics saying that Zelenskyy's proposal would only legitimize the moves that Russia had taken in Crimea and the Donets region.

When the COVID-19 pandemic spread through much of the world in 2020, the economic impact on Ukraine's businesses was particularly dire especially as lockdowns were imposed to keep the virus in check. In Donbas, where much of the conflict from Russian-supported separatists already had a detrimental effect on much of the infrastructure, the water supply was particularly affected during the pandemic.

Then, even while still reeling from the effects of COVID-19, Zelenskyy and the Ukrainian government had another looming crisis to deal with: in the latter months of 2021, Russian forces and military equipment were seen building up along the border, and joint military exercises with Belarus were also announced. Defense experts warned that Russia might be planning an invasion of Ukraine, and the world waited anxiously to see what would happen next.

CHAPTER 3

THE ESCALATION

Between the months of October and November in 2021, news outlets began reporting on the significant buildup of Russian military personnel and equipment taking place in key areas along the Ukrainian border. The activity immediately caught the attention of officials in Europe and the United States, and they sounded the alarm regarding the particularly concerning movements of Russian forces and equipment.

The development was of particular interest because in the months prior to the renewed buildup, Russian officials were already ramping up their stance on many issues related to Ukraine, including the increasingly closer ties of Ukraine with the West under the leadership of Zelenskyy. In some instances, Russia's Putin even went so far as to question the sovereignty of Ukraine. Another issue that Moscow was particularly averse to was the possibility of NATO expanding its presence in the region further by installing military infrastructure within Ukrainian territory.

Russia has always had a tense relationship with NATO. This comes as no surprise because the North Atlantic Treaty Organization was formed in 1949 specifically as a response to the Soviet Union's actions at the time, influencing countries around Eastern and Central Europe with Communist ideology and seeking to expand its network of satellite states in the region. The United States and its European allies formed NATO to hold off Soviet power; in turn, the Soviet Union and seven Eastern bloc states signed the Warsaw Pact in 1955.

Currently, there are thirty countries that are part of the NATO alliance. The 12 founding members from 1949 are all still part of the organization: the United Kingdom, the United States, Canada, Denmark, Belgium, Italy, Iceland, Luxembourg, the Netherlands, France, Portugal, and Norway. In addition, the alliance now includes Turkey, Greece, Spain, Germany, Hungary, Poland, Czech Republic, Estonia, Bulgaria, Lithuania, Latvia, Romania, Slovakia, Slovenia, Albania, Croatia, North Macedonia, and Montenegro.

Ukraine has indicated its desire to become part of NATO, along with Georgia and Bosnia and Herzegovina. Russia has been quite vocal in its opposition to Ukraine becoming a member of NATO, and it has repeatedly brought this up as justification for its military actions in negotiations with Ukraine. This is in spite of the fact that in the 1990s, there were a lot of speculations that Russia may eventually join NATO; however, its stance changed in the 2000s, and it positioned itself, yet again, on the opposite side of the alliance.

The relationship between NATO and Russia was particularly fractured during the Cold War. When Russia occupied and annexed the Crimean peninsula in 2014, its relationship with NATO soured further, and all cooperation between the two sides ground to a halt, despite communication channels still kept open. But why exactly is Putin so against the idea of Ukraine becoming part of NATO? After all, a number of countries that are also bordering Russia are already NATO members, namely Latvia and Estonia.

Jim Townsend, former deputy assistant secretary of defense for Europe and NATO under the administration of US President

Barack Obama, said in an interview with NPR, "The idea that Ukraine would actually establish relationships—like a nation would—to the European Union and NATO, that upsets in his mind this idea that Ukraine is Russia, Russia is Ukraine."

Meanwhile, former NATO official and Polish diplomat Robert Pszczel points to Putin's fascination with Russia's primary role in the global hierarchy as another reason why it views Ukraine's possible alliance with NATO as a problem. "He believes that Russia has the right, because it's a big power, to dictate to other countries. Just the very existence of NATO creates a problem for Putin because NATO stands for collective security and stands for upholding that international order," he said in an interview with NPR.

Over much of 2021, statements from Putin and other high-ranking officials of Russia regarding the increase of NATO presence and activities in Ukraine grew more ominous. In the past, Moscow's position was that if Ukraine became a bona fide member of NATO, they would not be able to abide by it. But in more recent statements, they have described it as a "red line" for relations between the two states.

In a July 2021 article, Putin alleged that Ukraine was being used by the Western alliance to build up anti-Russian sentiment in the region. "We will never allow our historical territories and people close to us living there to be used against Russia. And to those who will undertake such an attempt, I would like to say that this way they will destroy their own country," Putin wrote.

According to Putin, even though Ukraine is not yet an official NATO member, "military expansion on the territory is already underway, and this really poses a threat to the Russian Federation." He may have been referring to a number of joint exercises that Ukrainian forces have been participating in along with the United States and other NATO members since 2014, or the ongoing training of Ukrainian forces being conducted by US troops in the western part of the country for several years now.

But, it was not just the increasing cooperation of Ukraine with Western powers that Putin and Russia considered as reasons to flex military might and amass along the Ukrainian border. With the conflict in Donbas still not officially concluded, and continuing separatist movements from pro-Russia loyalists in key Ukraine regions, Russia declared itself as a peacekeeping force with the intention of maintaining order as two places in particular—Donetsk and Luhansk—established, self-proclaimed, people's republics, independent from Kyiv.

Russia also began dispatching military personnel to Belarus, declaring this as part of its joint exercises with the Belarusian military establishment. Additional forces were also sent to Transdniestria, a Russian-supported separatist region in Moldova, and in Crimea, currently annexed by Russia. According to estimates of Western defense analysts, as many as 190,000 Russian troops had been sent to the various strategic locations surrounding Ukraine, all ready for possible invasion.

Putin, however, continued to deny that he was planning to invade Ukraine, and dismissed the troop and equipment movements as just part of scheduled military exercises. On social media, videos showed Russian military trains and trucks transporting significant quantities of tanks, missiles, and other military hardware in western and southern Russia. Michael Kofman, director of the Russia studies program of CNA, a nonprofit analysis group, was skeptical of Russia's pronouncements. "The point is: It is not a drill. It doesn't appear to be a training exercise. Something is happening. What is it?" Kofman quipped.

It does appear that there were joint military exercises with Belarus back in September of 2021. The exercises, known as Zapad 2021, were conducted with personnel and equipment from both sides; however, what happened after the exercises was more suspicious to Western defense analysts. For instance, satellite imagery showed that Russia's 41st Combined Arms

Army did not return to its base in Novosibirsk, a city in Siberia, at the conclusion of Zapad 2021.

In addition to this, footage also showed the 1st Guards Tank Army, Russia's elite unit, moving its equipment and personnel from its base outside Moscow to key locations near Ukraine. Other training sites close to the Ukrainian border that were used during the Zapad 2021 exercises appeared to have large quantities of military equipment, control centers, and communication systems left intact by the Russians.

After the September 2021 joint exercises between Russia and Belarus, Oleksiy Danilov, the secretary of national security and defense council for Ukraine, estimated there were between 80,000 to 90,000 Russian troops already deployed along the border between Ukraine and Russia. This number did not include the thousands of soldiers who were already present in Crimea.

CNA's Kofman added that Russia also allocated a large budget in 2021 toward developing its military reserve, as well as for training its military personnel on anti-drone and anti-Javelin tactics. The anti-Javelin measures could be seen as a counter-preparation for the Ukrainian military's possession of Javelin anti-tank weapon systems, which were provided to the country by the United States in recent years.

As Russia's moves caused heightened tension in the region, US Secretary of Defense Lloyd Austin went on a trip to Ukraine in October of 2021. During the visit, Austin referred to Russia as a hindrance to peace, and also reiterated that NATO was still open to the possibility of Ukraine eventually becoming a full-fledged member. He added that no country can veto membership into the organization.

Meanwhile, Maria Zakharova, spokeswoman for the Russian Ministry of Foreign Affairs, alleged that Ukraine was drumming up plans to recapture the Donbas region by force. This mirrored a pronouncement from Dmitry Peskov, spokesman for the Kremlin, saying that the sales of Turkish drones to the Ukrainian government did not help the situation and led to further destabilization. Foreign ministry officials from Germany and France voiced concern about those drones, but Ukraine defended the move as part of its right to defend itself from Russia.

When pressed by journalists, Zelenskyy emphasized, "When the Ukrainian army feels the need to defend its land, it does so. And it will further act under this principle. We are not mounting an offensive, we are just responding," he said.

Also, Ukrainian Foreign Minister Dmytro Kuleba dismissed Russia's allegations that they were gearing up for military action in Donbas. "Russia is actively spreading fakes about Ukraine allegedly preparing an offensive or other nonsense. For the record, Ukraine does not prepare any offensive in the Donbas."

Kuleba also reiterated that it was, in fact, Russia that already prepositioned its personnel and military equipment very close to the Ukrainian border after the September joint exercises with Belarus, adding that the country "pulled back only a tiny part of the armada."

For weeks after Austin's visit to Ukraine, tension between Russia and Ukraine grew, and Russia continued to send tanks, artillery, air power, naval support, and military personnel close to the Ukrainian border. By late February of 2022, a few days before it started its offensive on Ukraine, around 190,000 Russian forces were already stationed along the border, ready for the imminent invasion.

The inevitability of the Russian attack became more apparent when Putin declared that Russia would recognize the Donetsk People's Republic and the Luhansk People's Republic, both self-declared, Russian-supported regions in the eastern side of Ukraine, as independent states. Donetsk and Luhansk were controlled by separatists loyal to Russia for close to eight years, and they held their own elections years ago declaring themselves to be separate from Ukraine. However, Putin only officially recognized their independent status in February 2022. Other countries that also recognized the two independent states were Venezuela, Nicaragua, Cuba, Syria, and the Georgia provinces of Abkhazia and South Ossetia.

Since Donetsk and Luhansk declared themselves separate from the central government of Kyiv in 2014, they have been able to gradually restore their desire to espouse a more Russian-style lifestyle in southeastern Ukraine. Much of that success, of course, has been due to the support provided by Russia itself, particularly in fending off loyal government forces. In these two People's Republics, the constitution of Josef Stalin has been adopted.

In the main square of Donetsk, there is a 13.5 meter statue of Vladimir Lenin, the founder of the Soviet Union, which clearly shows where the loyalty of much of this region lies. The death penalty is applied for several crimes, making these two areas (as well as Belarus) the only current places in Europe where capital punishment is practiced. Donetsk and Luhansk have become totalitarian areas very much akin to North Korea, and entry by foreigners has become close to impossible.

For Ukrainians who have relatives in Luhansk and Donetsk, visits are allowed but only if they travel by way of Russia first, which extends the travel time to up to 30 hours and at the cost of about $100, often including a lot of bribes along checkpoints and border patrols. Residents in the separatist republics are required to have a residency registration reminiscent of Soviet times.

Life in the People's Republics is very similar to how it was under Soviet rule. For instance, there are secret police monitoring residents' conversations, text messages, and phone calls, and any potential voices of dissent are quickly quelled. There have been reports of businessmen or citizens who have been detained in makeshift concentration camps or cellars when they refuse to donate their assets or other properties to the People's Republic's needs.

In an interview with Al Jazeera, Stanislave Aseyev, a publicist who was imprisoned in Donetsk in 2017 and sentenced to 15 years in jail for the charge of espionage by a separatist court, said, "It looks like the 1930s in the Soviet Union, a classic gulag." He was jailed and tortured in a Donetsk cellar for close to two years, until he was freed as part of a prisoner swap between the separatists and the loyalists.

Various human rights organizations and witnesses have called attention to the grave abuses and instances of torture happening in the cellars or concentration camps of Donetsk and Luhansk, where thousands of prisoners are still being held. In fact, many say that the human rights abuses happening currently in this separatist region are worse than the situation in Russia.

Ivar Dale, a senior policy adviser for the human rights group Norwegian Helsinki Committee, lamented, "The cellars where prisoners are held in Donetsk, and the widespread use of torture, are among the most obvious human rights issues. You could say that the political repression in Russia is doubly felt in Donetsk and Luhansk and other areas effectively under control of the Putin regime."

Apparently, the economic situation in this region has also deteriorated significantly, and the standard of living of average people in the People's Republics has taken a turn for the worse, exacerbated by the continuing conflict and the lack of stable economic ties to the outside world. Aseyev, the publicist who was imprisoned in Donetsk for two years, described life in these parts as "many times, if not dozens of times worse than in pre-war 2013."

What brought about this pro-Russian movement in this part of Ukraine? The events of the Ukrainian Revolution of Dignity can be seen as the main catalyst for the recent push back to the

Russian Federation, but a trip to the historical background can shed more light as to the affinity with Russia. Since the Soviet era, thousands of ethnic Russians resettled in the cities of Donetsk and Luhansk primarily due to the rich coal and iron ore deposits in the region. Thus, in these parts of Ukraine, the urban areas are mostly Russian-speaking.

In 2010, Donetsk native Viktor Yanukovych rose to power as the president of Ukraine, and he brought along with him a substantial number of his close associates and cronies to the central seat of power, Kyiv. His Russia-leaning moves as well as his controversial actions regarding the political and economic policies of Ukraine ignited the widespread protests that became known as the Revolution of Dignity, lasting from November of 2013 until February of the following year. The protests ended when Yanukovych was removed from office via a vote by the Ukrainian parliament.

Putin, on the other hand, condemned the Revolution of Dignity, referring to it as a "coup" against the legitimate government. The Kremlin then maneuvered its own provocations in the mostly Russian-speaking areas of eastern and southern Ukraine, calling this the Russian Spring and positioning the actions as liberation for the ethnic Russians in those areas. These led to pro-Russian uprisings and protest movements in the seaport of Odesa as well as Kharkiv, Ukraine's second-largest city. But both uprisings failed to topple forces loyal to Ukraine's central government.

As a result, thousands of volunteers who had come in from Russia headed to Donetsk and Luhansk to help out with the separatist uprisings already being carried out by local militia groups in those cities. Many local residents welcomed their presence, thinking that they will get justice for what they saw as an unjust ousting of Yanukovych. The conflict escalated, but soon enough Donetsk and Luhansk came under the control of pro-Russian separatists, and independent republics were then installed.

To date, Ukraine does not recognize the validity of the People's Republics of Donetsk and Luhansk. The majority of the world's countries also do not recognize them as independent states. Officially, Ukraine has also cut off economic ties to the two separatist regions, although there have been under-the-table deals and back-channel coordinations. Still, for the most part, the economic backbone of the two separatist republics comes from the billions of dollars sent each year by Russia in order to support the territories.

Considering that Russia is actually bleeding a large amount of money every year to support the People's Republics, Putin may have very specific economic goals in mind behind his decision to launch an offensive beyond the Donbas region and into other parts of Ukraine. Aleksey Kusch, an analyst based in Kyiv, told Al Jazeera that Putin's end game in Donbas may be "very simple—to lower the price tag of maintaining the occupied territories."

Another way Moscow can decrease the cost of bankrolling the separatist regions would be to eliminate the numerous middlemen who were able to keep a big chunk of the profits from coal and steel exports in the region, and even profited substantially from the humanitarian aid that reached Donbas and somehow ended up getting resold illegally on the black market. Kusch told Al Jazeera, "They kept up to 70 percent of the profits."

Still, most experts and insiders with full knowledge of the situation do agree that it is Putin's concern about NATO's increasing presence in the region and his belief that Ukraine is, at the end of the day, part of Russia, that is driving this decision to launch a military offensive. In fact, in dialogues held between Russia and its Western counterparts, Moscow has repeatedly insisted that it wants guarantees that Ukraine will be permanently prohibited from becoming a member of NATO. Russia also wants NATO to immediately stop all forms of military activities in eastern Europe because, in its eyes,

NATO is undermining the security situation in this part of the world.

NATO's leaders, however, have refused to give in to Russia's demands, and have countered that Russia does not have the right to veto the foreign policy decisions of a sovereign state such as Ukraine. NATO has also brandished its open door policy, emphasizing that any European country has the right to request membership into the alliance.

Although NATO has reiterated since 2008 that it is open to giving Ukraine the opportunity to become a member, the alliance has yet to formalize the membership. This is in spite of increased cooperation between Ukraine and NATO in the past few years, and especially as the war with Russia took place in 2022. For many of the Western countries in the alliance, Ukraine still has much to prove in terms of eliminating corruption in its government system, as well as in satisfying various other requirements in terms of economic, military, and political criteria based on the 1995 Study on Enlargement.

Another major factor that may be delaying the formalization of Ukraine's entry into NATO is the ongoing conflict with Russia. Many of the NATO members may be concerned that accepting Ukraine at this time may not bode well with their individual and collective relations with Russia. It would, perhaps, put them in direct conflict with Putin, especially considering the collective defense principle. In order for any country to be accepted into NATO, all of the 30 member countries must unanimously approve the proposal.

Putin is dead set against the idea of Ukraine becoming a NATO member, and sees the possibility of Ukraine joining NATO as a continued wave of expansion of Western powers into the region that, in his mind, should be more under Moscow's influence. He also believes that the Western powers have somehow betrayed him and have reneged on verbal promises they made towards the end of the Cold War that NATO would not continue its eastward expansion. NATO, of course, has denied that it made any such verbal commitment.

With all of these factors contributing to the simmering tensions in the region, the stage was set for what would be the most significant military clash of 2022 so far. Much of the world's attention would soon be peeled away from the continuing effects of the COVID-19 pandemic and move instead toward the Russo-Ukrainian War, complete with all the elements of a classic David-versus-Goliath saga. Now, a smaller but determined Ukrainian army and civilian population is determined to fight back against the larger, more sophisticated Russian forces.

CHAPTER 4

THE INVASION

On the 24th of February, 2022, what many had feared would happen finally came to pass: Russia began its invasion of Ukraine. This became the latest and most significant escalation of the ongoing Russo-Ukrainian War which started back in 2014 when Russia occupied the Crimean peninsula. Towards the last few months of 2021, world leaders and international observers were already sounding the alarm regarding the movement of massive numbers of Russian troops and military equipment along the Ukrainian border, and were warning that Putin was planning to attack sometime soon.

Russian officials repeatedly denied that there were any plans to attack or invade Ukraine, despite the movement of their forces and equipment close to the border. But on February 21st, 2022, the inevitability of war became all too clear as Russia officially recognized the Donetsk People's Republic and the Luhansk People's Republic. These two self-proclaimed separatists states located in the Donbas region of Ukraine had been taken over and controlled by pro-Russia forces since 2014, and were widely believed to be supported by Russia financially and militarily.

After the announcement of Russia's recognition of the legitimacy of the two republics, the Federation Council of

Russia officially authorized the utilization of military force overseas, thus giving way for Russian troops to begin entering the territories. The request came from Russian President Vladimir Putin and was approved by the upper house of the Russian parliament. Even before the official announcement, there were already reports that Russian troops were already present in some areas held by rebels in eastern Ukraine, and the authorization was just a formality for all intents and purposes.

After this development, international condemnation was swift, and most countries were in agreement that Russia's move was an act of aggression against Ukraine. The United States also changed its tone and started referring to Russia's actions and deployment of troops in eastern Ukraine as an invasion. Initially, the United States had been hesitant to use the term, and President Joe Biden had made a pronouncement that an invasion would trigger severe and far-reaching sanctions against Russia.

Joe Finer, the principal deputy national security adviser for the United States, was one of the first in the Biden administration to officially refer to it as an invasion when he said, "We think this is, yes, the beginning of an invasion, Russia's latest invasion into Ukraine. An invasion is an invasion and that is what is underway."

A US official speaking anonymously said that the White House made the decision to label Russia's moves as an "invasion" of Ukraine because of the developments happening on the ground. The official added that the Biden administration wanted to see first what Russia's actions would be, particularly with regard to troop movements in the region.

Although Western powers were united in condemning Putin's actions, the words they used in the initial days after Russia's attacks varied significantly in tone and severity. European Union Foreign Policy Chief Josep Borrell told the press in France, "Russian troops have entered in Donbas. We consider

Donbas part of Ukraine." When he was pressed further, Borrell added, "I wouldn't say that it is a fully-fledged invasion, but Russian troops are on Ukrainian soil."

Spanish Foreign Minister Jose Manuel Albares was also quite measured in his statement, and emphasized instead that "if Russia uses force against Ukraine, sanctions will be massive." Meanwhile, British Health Secretary Sajid Javid was more forthcoming, and referred to the development on Sky News as "the invasion of Ukraine." The Defense Ministry of Poland also referred to it as an invasion from the beginning.

Sanctions against Russia were swiftly imposed by various countries as the invasion on Ukraine began. Top-level officials of the European Union were quick to announce that the bloc would be meeting regarding what sanctions to impose on a number of Russian officials and banking institutions, in a move that would limit their access to capital and global financial markets.

Meanwhile, British Prime Minister Boris Johnson also announced that the United Kingdom would immediately impose economic sanctions on at least five Russian banks and three wealthy Russian citizens, while stating that if Russia continues with a full-scale offensive against Ukraine, the United Kingdom would consider "further powerful sanctions."

The United States immediately suspended investment and trade with the separatist republics via an executive order from the White House. Other measures and economic sanctions, as well as travel restrictions, would soon be announced by the United States against a significant number of Russian financial institutions and wealthy businessmen.

Perhaps one of the most significant responses in the early days of Russia's invasion of Ukraine was Germany's decision to suspend the certification process of the Nord Stream 2 pipeline. The suspension was announced by German Chancellor Olaf Scholz as a punitive measure of Germany against Russia's actions, specifically Moscow's decision to recognize the separatist republics in Donbas, which Scholz described as a "serious break of international law."

Speaking to the press in Berlin, Scholz also reiterated, "Now it's up to the international community to react to this one-sided, incomprehensible, and unjustified action by the Russian president." Scholz also emphasized that the moves were needed to "send a clear signal to Moscow that such actions won't remain without consequences."

The Nord Stream 2 pipeline was a major project that was specifically designed to supply natural gas from Russia into Germany, with the goal of helping to meet the energy needs of Germany, especially as it prepares to halt the operations of its remaining three nuclear power plants reducing its dependence on coal. For many years, the United States and other European countries have been vocal in calling for Germany to halt the project. The United States, in particular, had insisted that the project would increase Europe's dependence on Russian energy, but Germany appeared to be steadfast in its commitment to the Nord Stream 2 project, at least until this Ukraine crisis commenced.

Currently, about half of the natural gas supply in Germany comes from Russia, and it is expected that reliance on natural gas will increase in the coming years. Natural gas is used for about ¼ of the country's energy needs, and with the phase out of nuclear power and coal, in alignment with the country's goal of ending all fossil fuel use by 2045, natural gas will exponentially increase in use. This is why the Nord Stream 2 project was defended for a long time by the German government, despite pressure from other countries.

Following up on the decision to suspend the certification process, Scholz told the media, "The situation now is fundamentally different. That may sound technical, but it's a necessary administrative step without which the certification of the pipeline cannot happen now."

In response to the announcement, Ukraine's Foreign Minister Dmytro Kuleba lauded Germany's decision to suspend the certification of the Nord Stream 2 pipeline, writing on Twitter, "This is a morally, politically, and practically correct step in the current circumstances. True leadership means tough decisions in difficult times. Germany's move proves just that."

But former Russian president Dmitry Medvedev, who is also the current deputy chair of the Security Council of Russia, condemned the decision saying, "Welcome to the brave new world where Europeans are very soon going to pay 2,000 Euros for 1,000 cubic meters of natural gas!"

Meanwhile in Ukraine, President Volodymyr Zelenskyy recalled the Ukrainian ambassador to Moscow soon after Russia's recognition of the separatist republics. Zelenskyy also said that he is seriously considering breaking all diplomatic ties with Russia. He appeared on Ukrainian television that evening and tried to calm the fears of the country, saying, "We are not afraid of anyone or anything. We don't owe anyone anything. And we won't give anything to anyone."

Diplomatic attempts by various Western leaders meeting with Russian counterparts soon bogged down, and Putin appeared on television in the early morning hours of February 24th officially declaring war. Soon after, Russian forces began to attack Ukraine from at least three fronts, making this the largest military attack on any European state since World War II. Throughout the day, there were reports of gunfire and explosions in multiple areas around Ukraine, including the capital Kyiv. At least 70 people were reported to have died during the first day of the invasion.

Late in the day, Zelenskyy announced a general mobilization among Ukrainian citizens to be carried out within the next three months in order "to ensure the defense of the state." He called on Ukrainians to stand up and fight for the sovereignty of their country, a call that was heeded by thousands of civilians who began to take up arms and improvise what resources they have to hold back the Russian invaders.

Fierce fighting between Russian and Ukrainian forces was reported all around the various fronts of the conflict, including in several areas close to Kyiv. The Hostomel Airport adjacent to Kyiv was the scene of intense fighting as Russian paratroopers landed and attempted to capture it, although a Ukrainian official later noted that they were able to recapture the facility. Intense fighting was also reported in the northeast regions of Sumy and Kharkiv, as well as the southern region of Kherson.

Russian forces, meanwhile, were able to take control of the former nuclear power plant of Chernobyl, which is situated 90 kilometers or 60 miles north of the capital. It was a significant development because the Chernobyl Nuclear Power Plant is strategically located along the quickest road from Kyiv to Belarus—a close ally of Russia where many troops were already positioned. Russian forces continued to move closer to Kyiv, although the Ukrainian side was able to put up a gallant stand and hold back the invaders.

As the invasion commenced, thousands of Ukrainian residents began to flee to other parts of the country as well as across the border to neighboring countries in order to escape the fighting. Roads leading out of Kyiv, particularly the highway toward the west, was congested with heavy traffic, making evacuation more problematic. The refugee agency of the United Nations reported that about 100,000 Ukrainians had fled from their residences within the first few days of the conflict, with many crossing over to Poland, Hungary, Romania, and Moldova.

Zelenskyy was resolute in rallying Ukrainian soldiers and civilians to do their part in defending Ukrainian territory, and he also said arms would be given to all citizens who are willing to take part in the defense of the country. As Russian missiles began to fall all around Ukrainian targets and thousands of Russian forces entered Ukrainian soil, Zelenskyy referred to the events as the rise of a new *Iron Curtain*.

"What we have heard today are not just missile blasts, fighting, and the rumble of aircraft. This is the sound of a new Iron Curtain, which has come down and is closing Russia off from the civilized world," according to Zelenskyy.

Meanwhile, Putin also gave a dire warning to Ukraine, as well as to any country that would help them, alluding to the nuclear arms in Russia's arsenal. "Whoever tries to hinder us… should know that Russia's response will be immediate. And it will lead you to such consequences that you have never encountered in your history," Putin declared.

More sanctions and measures were announced by major world powers. Soon after a consultation with the Group of Seven industrialized countries, Biden announced that measures will be implemented to hinder Russia from being able to access or do business using the major world currencies, and he also slapped sanctions on a number of Russian-owned businesses and banks. The United Kingdom moved to impose limits on Russian banks and key cronies of Putin, while the EU leaders moved to freeze Russian assets all across the 27 member-states.

By early March 2022, Russia's military campaign was able to close in on Kyiv and Mariupol. The city of Mariupol is about 600 kilometers northwest of Kyiv, so it is not immediately clear as to why Russian forces are intent on capturing the city. If Russia is able to overtake Mariupol, it will not likely affect the outcome of the war either way. Along with the increased offensive on the two cities, Russia also stepped up their advance across Kherson to Mykolayiv, and the Zaporizhya Nuclear Power Plant located north of Crimea was captured by Russian forces.

The extent of Russia's military operations in Ukraine included infantry divisions backed up by armored units and air support in the eastern part of Ukraine, while missile attacks were the initial offensive in the western part. Then, both infantry and tank attacks were launched towards Kyiv, from Crimea in the south, from the southeastern portion originating in Luhansk and Donbas, and from the eastern side. By the middle of March, a perimeter had been successfully formed by Russian forces, surrounding Kyiv, Mariupol, Luhansk, Donbas, and a number of other very important cities.

What Russia did not anticipate, or may have underestimated, was the resilience and determination by which Ukrainian armed forces and civilians were able to withstand the attacks and keep the invaders from capturing key cities. Russia may have expected push back from Ukraine, but the extent by which the smaller country was able to fight back was quite surprising, even to the rest of the world watching the conflict unfold.

Within the first few days of the Russian incursion, there were already a number of reports of significant wins of Ukrainian forces against their Russian counterparts, including several Russian warplanes and military helicopters shot down. In Kharkiv, Ukrainian troops were able to mount a successful counterattack and capture Russian armored vehicles and weapons.

The war plan of Putin did not take into account the fierce resistance from the Ukrainian side, as he had assumed that the might and sophistication of Russia's armed forces would swiftly pound Ukraine's inferior army into submission. The plan was for the tanks to enter from multiple fronts, and paratroopers to capture key installations around the capital, with the final part of the operation being the capture of Kyiv—the seat of the government.

Putin may have also assumed that the majority of Ukrainians would simply adjust to the new life and play along for fear of arrest, imprisonment, or execution. He was also bent on installing a puppet government loyal to Russia, similar to the situation in Crimea and Eastern Ukraine. While the might of Russia's military did succeed in capturing significant portions of the southern and the southeastern Ukraine, including Kherson, the reaction from the locals was not one of passive acceptance, but active resistance and protest.

When Russian forces seized Kherson and most of its surrounding area, local residents took to the streets in droves, protesting in the main square without showing any fear of being shot by the soldiers, waving Ukrainian flags while holding peaceful but noisy demonstrations. Residents even succeeded in hijacking an armored carrier used by the Russian military and proudly took the vehicle around the city streets to the adulation of the protesters. Other massive anti-Russia protests also broke out in Melitopol, despite the threat from Russian troops firing shots into the air, as well as Berdyansk, a seaport community in Azov.

The resilience of the Ukrainian defense and fighting spirit captivated the eyes and hearts of the world. United States Secretary of State Antony Blinken said over the BBC that the Russian invasion looked to be faltering, and even stated his belief that Ukraine "can absolutely win against Russia." Blinken also added, "The war has already not gone as Russian President Vladimir Putin might have planned."

Another US official who spoke to Reuters anonymously pointed out, "Ukrainians still have a significant majority of their air combat power available to them, both fixed-wing and rotary wing as well as unmanned systems and surface-to-air systems." Two weeks into the Russian invasion, it appeared that Ukrainian aircraft were still fully operational along with a number of their air defense systems, and this scenario had been considered highly unlikely when the incursion began. Most had expected Ukraine's defense to last only a few days once the Russians commenced their operation.

Things took a dire turn, however, as Russia began to realize that its original plans of land invasion were not going according to plan, and frustration mounted as the troops tried but failed to overtake Kyiv. Russian forces began to target civilians, indiscriminately shelling neighborhoods and bombing structures. Civilian casualties continued to mount in a number of Ukrainian cities, such as Bila Tserkva, Kharkiv, and Bucha.

In Mariupol, thousands of people were trapped amidst intense fighting and almost non-stop shelling from Russian forces. There were about 200,000 residents unable to escape from Mariupol when an agreement between the two countries to provide a humanitarian corridor for civilians to escape did not materialize. Without electricity, water, and heat, the situation turned from bad to worse for the residents of Mariupol.

Speaking to the *Observer*, one volunteer fighter, Anatoliy Lozar, described the difficult circumstances the trapped residents were experiencing. "Everything has been hit. Apartment blocks, shops, the hospital. It's like World War II... I saw a car pull up outside a hospital and a mother run out with a wounded child. I have no idea whether the child lived or died. We can't even collect our dead. The morgue has no electricity."

Still, Lozar was determined to keep fighting, echoing what many Ukrainians in Mariupol and across the country were also feeling. "We won't give up. We will fight to the very last man."

The mayor of Mariupol, Vadym Boychenko, lamented how Russian armed forces were indiscriminately shelling hospitals and residential neighborhoods. "They want to wipe Mariupol and Mariupol residents off the face of the Earth," the mayor said, adding that the city's food supplies had reached a critical low. Even medicines and other first aid and essential supplies were running out, according to Medecins Sans Frontieres. City residents had to drink rainwater and snow because potable water was no longer available.

Still, despite the seemingly insurmountable challenges, Ukraine kept fighting on and pushing the Russian invaders back as much as they could, adding to the increasing frustration of Putin and his cohorts in Moscow regarding the progress and pace of the offensive. Speaking to the *Observer*, Andrei Soldatov, an expert on the Russian security services, described Russia's armed forces as seemingly not in control of the situation. "You have the political element dominating decision-making," he said.

Meanwhile, Olena Chebeluik, a historian from the city of Lviv, attributed the surprising resistance to the outdated hardware still being utilized by the Russian forces. "Russia has a 20th-century army. Ukraine is using 21st-century weapons," she said. "We are fighting in small mobile groups. Our fighters can hide. They know the territory. Locals support them."

Ukraine also capitalized on the increasingly low morale and lack of proper preparation among the Russian reserve units. The loss of the Moskva, the huge flagship of Russia's Black Sea fleet named after the capital city, struck yet another blow to the pride of the Russians. Outside a recruitment office in Lviv, instructor Vitaly Glyuk described how their enemies were getting tired of the conflict: "The Russians are getting a bit exhausted and now we are going forward. It's our time. We have been fighting this monster for 300 years already."

There was even an optimism among Ukrainians that this resistance could lead to the recapture of Crimea, the peninsula which had been annexed by Russia in 2014. Glyuk exclaimed, "Once we have won back our territory in the south we will get Crimea as well."

As millions of Ukrainians fled the fighting, thousands more stayed behind, ready to battle for their sovereignty. Even more impressive to watch was the number of Ukrainians who had been living overseas returning to the country, ready to take up arms and fight alongside the armed forces and the civilian volunteers. By mid-March, Ukrainian defense minister Oleksii Reznikov announced that more than 66,000 Ukrainians from abroad had come back to fight. "Ukrainians, we are invincible!" Reznikov enthused.

It cannot be denied that one of the biggest boosts to the morale and willingness of the Ukrainian citizenry to fight for their country was no less than their president, Volodymyr Zelenskyy. The comedian-turned-president made a vow to continue fighting the Russian forces, staying behind in the capital to lead in the frontlines, much to the amazement and admiration of his citizens and the whole world.

A couple of days after Russia started attacking Ukraine, Zelenskyy shot a video from outside his office in the capital, promising to lead the fight and protect Kyiv and the rest of the country from the invaders. "I am here. We will not lay down any weapons. We will defend our state, because our weapons are our truth," he declared.

He also reminded Ukrainians not to believe any of the misleading information going around that Ukrainian armed forces have already surrendered. "A lot of fake information has appeared on the Internet saying that I allegedly called on our army to lay down its arms and that evacuation is underway. Our truth is that this is our land, our country, our children, and we will protect all of this. This is what I wanted to tell you. Glory to Ukraine!" Zelenskyy emphatically said in the video clip.

It was not the first time that Zelenskyy was seen on video from the embattled capital, and neither would it be the last. As Russian missiles started raining down all around Ukraine, he refused to leave Kyiv, and chose to stay alongside the forces who remained to protect the capital. In another video circulated online, he said, "Many cities in our country are under attack. Chernihiv, Sumy, Kharkiv, our guys and girls in Donbas, the cities of southern Ukraine and especially Kyiv. We cannot lose the capital."

Zelenskyy spoke like a war general, boosting the morale of Ukrainian fighters and calling on everyone to stand their ground. "I address our defenders. On all fronts tonight, the enemy will use all of its forces at disposal to break our resistance, dishonorably, cruelly, and inhumanely. Tonight they will go on assault. We must all understand what awaits us," he announced.

The Ukrainian president was also resolute in calling for Western nations to come to Ukraine's aid and impose heavier sanctions and measures against Russia. Zelenskyy kept in constant communication with NATO leaders, including US President Joe Biden, French President Emmanuel Macron, and German Chancellor Olaf Scholz, all of whom pledged to provide more support and ramp up sanctions against Putin.

The transformation of Volodymyr Zelenskyy into a revered and inspirational world leader is truly one for the books. Just three years ago, he was more popularly known in Ukraine for playing the role of a president in a popular comedy series on television. Then, in 2019, the lawyer-turned-entertainer rose to power and was elected president of a country facing a number of challenges, external conflicts, and internal tensions.

Zelenskyy was often criticized early on in his presidency for downplaying the looming threat of a Russian invasion, as he often appeared too relaxed or calm when pressed about Russia's movements close to the Ukrainian border. He was also widely lambasted for failing to put an end to the conflict in Eastern Ukraine, which was one of his biggest campaign promises. The conflict escalated, eventually leading to Russia recognizing the separatist republics and ushering in the eventual invasion.

But as the diplomatic channels started closing one by one, and it became clear that Russia was bent on encroaching into Ukrainian soil and escalating the war, Zelenskyy's tone changed from calm to serious, and his demeanor also began to reflect Ukraine's willingness to fight off any threats to its sovereignty.

Valentyn Gladkykh, a political analyst based in Kyiv, said in an interview with NBC News that when Zelenskyy's performance in the final weeks leading to the invasion was assessed, he truly shone through as a commander-in-chief and was able to take on the role of wartime leader with much confidence, which is why the Ukrainian population has also been buoyed into supporting him and defending the country.

Gladkykh said, "No Ukrainian president has ever dealt with a full-on invasion. Having encountered the unprecedented threat, Zelenskyy has shown his best side."

Whether Zelenskyy's masterful showing as a leader in a time of crisis will be enough to propel Ukraine to win against Putin and his forces remains to be seen as the conflict continues to unfold. Although Ukraine has been able to defend much of its territory, it is still an uphill climb as the country is facing the massive army of Russia, which is one of the largest worldwide. Ukraine's armed forces are outnumbered and outgunned, and the advantage is clearly on Russia's side when it comes to military might and size.

What has been instrumental in Ukraine's fight for its sovereignty is the assistance that many countries around the world have continued to send. Although NATO and other democratic powers have not sent troops on the ground to fight alongside Ukrainian forces, averting a full-on global war with Russia, they have been more than willing to send other forms of support to Ukraine as it battles Putin's troops. Within a few days after the beginning of the invasion, the United States Department of State was instructed by Biden to release an additional $350 million worth of weapons to Ukraine, allocated through the Foreign Assistance Act.

The additional $350 million worth of weapons from the US was separate from the more than $1 billion security assistance to

Ukraine given over the last 12 months. According to the Pentagon, the weapons shipment included small arms, anti-armor, body armor, various types of munitions, and anti-aircraft systems.

Leaders of the European Union, meanwhile, agreed to send $502 million worth of weapons to Ukraine. It was the first time that the EU financed an arms purchase and delivery in its history. In addition to this collective support, European Union foreign policy head Josep Borrell added that a number of nations have also committed to send fighter jets to Ukrainian armed forces to assist in their operations.

As early as January, the United Kingdom already announced that it was supporting Ukraine militarily. At that time, Defense Secretary Ben Wallace said the United Kingdom had come to "the decision to supply Ukraine with light anti-armor defensive weapon systems." When the invasion broke out, the British government ramped up military support for Ukraine's forces, and they sent more equipment and lethal defensive weapons.

Prime Minister Johnson said in front of the parliament, "In light of the increasingly threatening behavior from Russia and in line with our previous support, the UK will shortly be providing a further package of military support to Ukraine. This will include lethal aid in the form of defensive weapons and non-lethal aid."

France, for its part, was one of the first European countries to deliver defensive anti-aircraft systems and digital weapons to Ukraine, in response to Kyiv's requests. The French government also announced that it will be sending more military equipment, weapons, and fuel supplies to Ukrainian fighters.

Early on in the conflict, the Netherlands was also quick to come to Ukraine's aid. The Dutch government coursed letters to its parliament announcing that it was responding to Ukraine's requests for help, and sent 200 Stinger air defense rockets, 50

Panzerfaust 3 anti-tank weapons, 400 rockets, and other equipment within the first week of the war.

Germany has always maintained a policy against weapons exports to war-torn areas or conflict zones, but it abandoned this policy and announced that it was also supplying Ukraine with 1,000 anti-tank weapons and 500 Stinger surface-to-air missiles. In relation to the pledged support, German Chancellor Olaf Scholz said, "The Russian invasion of Ukraine marks a turning point. It is our duty to do our best to support Ukraine in defending itself against Putin's invading army."

Two other historically neutral European nations, Sweden and Finland, decided to break their usual stances and support Ukraine. Sweden sent 5,000 anti-tank weapons, while Finland delivered 1,500 rocket launchers, 2,500 assault rifles, 150,000 ammunition rounds, and 70,000 field ration servings. Other European nations followed suit, with Denmark sending an additional 2,700 anti-tank weapons, Norway delivering 2,000 M72 anti-tank weapons and numerous body armor and helmets, and Belgium supplying 3,000 automatic rifles, 200 anti-tank weapons, and an additional 3,800 tons of fuel.

Within the first few days of the invasion of Ukraine, Portugal also sent helmets, grenades, automatic G3 rifles, ammunition, bulletproof vests, and night-vision goggles for the Ukrainian fighters, while Spain supplied 1,370 grenade launchers, 700,000 munitions, and automatic weapons. Greece also pledged both humanitarian aid and defense supplies; incidentally, there is a significant Greek community in Ukraine, and several Greek citizens have been reported killed in the conflict.

Romania, which is Ukraine's next door neighbor, opened up its 11 military hospitals for the treatment of people who were injured in the crisis. The country also sent fuel supplies, helmets, bulletproof vests, and other military equipment totalling $3.3 million. Meanwhile, the Czech Republic announced that it would be immediately sending 4,000 mortars,

30,000 pistols, 7,000 assault rifles, 3,000 machine guns, one million bullets, and an undisclosed number of sniper rifles, on top of $1.6 million dollars worth of mortars already pledged.

Many countries around the world also immediately offered other forms of aid to Ukraine, particularly to address the unfolding humanitarian crisis as the conflict drags on. According to data from the Council on Foreign Relations released in the last week of March 2022, around ten million Ukrainians, or about a fourth of the total population of the country, had been displaced because of the Russian attacks. Of this number, four million Ukrainians have escaped to neighboring countries such as Poland, Hungary, and Moldova.

Meanwhile, the United Nations estimates that there may be close to seven million internally displaced persons and up to seven million refugees because of the Ukraine crisis. These sobering numbers would make this the single largest war-related mass migration since the 1990s, when the Balkan Wars took place. An additional concern is the relatively low COVID-19 vaccination rate of Ukraine; only an estimated 36% of the Ukrainian population has been fully vaccinated against the virus, and with the health services and hospitals already stretched to their limits, COVID-19 treatment could be difficult for the citizens to access.

About half of Ukrainian refugees have been received in neighboring Poland, which was already the home of around 1.5 million Ukrainians prior to the conflict. As of the last week of March, more than 2.2 million refugees from Ukraine were already in Poland; the country had already prepared for the situation by prepositioning temporary shelters, hospitals, and reception centers with information, medical supplies, and food items.

Other refugees are currently in Belarus, Moldova, Hungary, Slovakia, Romania, and other European countries, while an estimated 271,000 people escaped to Russia. The Czech

Republic suspended its entry ban and COVID-19 restrictions to accommodate refugees from the conflict zones, while Ireland waived all visa requirements for Ukrainians.

Apart from the individual measures that countries in Europe started taking early on to accept the millions of refugees coming out of Ukraine, the European Union also activated its own plan to help with the refugee evacuation. European Union officials supported the activation of the Temporary Protection Directive, a law that had never before been used by the bloc prior to this time. Under this law, refugees escaping from Ukraine would be allowed to enter any of the member states of the European Union for up to three years, and they would not need to apply for asylum within this time period. This was in addition to the greater freedoms already given to Ukrainians to enter the EU; since 2017, Ukrainian citizens have been allowed to enter European Union countries without any visa requirements.

Within days of Russia's invasion of Ukraine, a number of agencies of the United Nations started to take action and assist with humanitarian efforts. UN Secretary-General Antonio Guterres assigned a crisis coordinator in charge of Ukraine, and he also announced that an initial $20 million worth of aid would be released from the UN Central Emergency Response Fund. An additional $1.7 billion was set as the goal to be raised by the UN refugee agency specifically for humanitarian aid.

Incidentally, the UN Security Council had a meeting on February 25th to discuss a US-led resolution that strongly condemned Russia's actions and called on Putin to withdraw forces immediately from Ukrainian territory. Eleven of the fifteen Security Council members favored the resolution, while India, China, and the United Arab Emirates abstained from voting. Russia, as a member of the Security Council, not unsurprisingly, vetoed the resolution, and the measure was blocked because of this.

One week later, the full UN General Assembly held an emergency session to discuss the war between Russia and Ukraine. This would be the first full assembly since 1997. In this session, the Assembly voted 141 to five in favor of a very similar resolution, denouncing Russia's war against Ukraine. Most of the world was united in condemnation of Putin and his acts of aggression.

The common thread in the worldwide response to the crisis has been guarded support of Ukraine, carefully measured so as to avoid triggering further conflict and igniting a global war against Russia. One such example is the response from Turkey. The Turkish Foreign Ministry denounced Russia's recognition of the separatist republics in Ukraine, and President Recep Tayyip Erdogan was vocal in his opposition to any violation of the territorial sovereignty of Ukraine. But, when Zelenskyy requested Turkey to restrict the waterways of the Black Sea to Russian troops, Turkey thumbed down the plea, saying that it "cannot stop Russian warships accessing the Black Sea via its straits, as Ukraine has requested, due to a clause in an international pact."

A few weeks later, Turkey did close the Black Sea, this time restricting all maritime traffic in the waterway—not just Russian warships. It reiterated that the closure of the Black Sea was stipulated in the 1936 Montreux Convention which effectively allows Turkey to restrict movement through Dardanelles and Bosporus during war time.

Israel is another country that has towed the line somewhat in its response to the Russia-Ukraine crisis. On February 23rd, the Foreign Ministry of Israel released a statement supporting the territorial integrity of Ukraine, but with no explicit mention of Russia. The following day, Israeli Prime Minister Naftali Bennett declared solidarity with Ukrainians but steered clear of any mention of territorial integrity or condemnation of Russia. In stark contrast, Israeli Foreign Minister Yair Lapid was forthcoming in calling Russia's actions "a grave violation of the international order."

In several other instances, Prime Minister Bennett and even President Isaac Herzog all expressed support for Ukraine without condemning Russia. Even when a Russian air strike hit the Babyn Yar Holocaust Memorial in Ukraine on March 2nd, Herzog was still careful with his words, referring to the war as a violation of international law, but without explicitly calling out Russia. "This attack sums up the terrible tragedy we are witnessing, which has been unravelling before our very eyes," Herzog said.

The government of Syria, a long-term ally of Russia, approved of Russia's recognition of the separatist republics of Donetsk and Luhansk. Prior to the invasion, the Office of the Presidency already released a statement saying that Syria is "prepared to work to build relations with the republics of Luhansk and Donetsk and to strengthen relations in the context of common interests and mutual respect." A day after the start of the invasion, Syrian state media reported that President Bashar al-Assad personally called Putin expressing his approval of the actions, calling them a "correction of history and a rebalance to the world... lost after the dissolution of the Soviet Union."

Assad added that "Syria supports the Russian Federation, based on its conviction of its correct stance that repelling NATO expansion is Russia's right." Assad went further with this claim and took a shot at the Western bloc, saying, "Western countries bear responsibility for chaos and bloodshed as a result of their policies aimed at controlling peoples, as these countries use their dirty methods to support terrorists in Syria and the Nazis in Ukraine and in various parts of the world."

Iranian President Ebrahim Raisi echoed Assad's sentiments, blaming NATO and the West for the escalation. Raisi said to Putin, "NATO expansion is a serious threat to the stability and security of independent countries in different regions." Other officials of Iran also placed the blame squarely on Western countries; a tweet from Iran's Foreign Minister Hossein Amir-Abdollahian read, "The Ukraine crisis is rooted in NATO's provocations."

Across the Middle East, however, there has been more disapproval of Putin's actions against Ukraine. The United Arab Emirates, Iraq, Libya, and Lebanon have all refused to recognize the legitimacy of the breakaway republics, and have called on both Russia and Ukraine to resolve the conflict as soon as possible and exert diplomatic solutions. Similar calls for restraint have been issued by Bahrain, Tunisia, Kuwait, Oman, and Saudi Arabia.

But as the war between Russia and Ukraine escalated, international observers were waiting to see what China's stance and actions would be. China has maintained friendlier relations with Russia over the years, and many were monitoring whether China would position itself with Russia or the West in the midst of this crisis. In this situation, however, it seems China has found itself in a predicament where it needs to find a delicate balance in order to protect its interests.

While China's diplomatic relationship with Russia has become closer in recent times, and Beijing is keen to shore up its strategic and military ties with Moscow, it also has to avoid being seen as a supporter of war in Europe, particularly because many of its biggest economic and trading partners are on the continent. If China is perceived as a fervent supporter of Russia's war on Ukraine, there could be major trade repercussions particularly from wealthy countries in Western Europe and North America.

When the United Nations Security Council met in order to vote on the resolution condemning Russia's invasion of Ukraine, many had expected China to side with Russia and vote against the measure. But China made a surprising move, choosing instead to abstain from the vote and maintaining its noninterference policy. While some analysts already consider this as a minor win for the Western bloc, China still has not come out and directly condemned Russia's actions, so it remains to be seen where China's sympathy really lies in the conflict.

Another major point of discussion that has come up in the midst of these developments is China's own tensioned relationship with Taiwan, a self-governing island that China insists is a rogue province that should be unified with its mainland government soon. On social media, Chinese nationalists are calling for China to essentially mimic what Russia has done to Ukraine and reclaim its own separatist region. But so far, Chinese Premier Xi Jinping has been careful about his statements, and the Chinese government knows that how it handles the Ukrainian conflict will have repercussions on its place in the global stage.

In Taiwan, the government and its citizens are closely watching the events, and the ever-present threat of an invasion by China is on the back of everyone's minds. In the hours after Putin's forces started attacking Ukraine, Taiwan was quick to proclaim its solidarity with Ukraine, and it also imposed a number of economic sanctions on Russia. Lai Ching-te, vice-president of Taiwan, said, "The principle of self-determination cannot be erased by brute force."

Taiwan also went on high alert soon after the escalation in eastern Europe, with President Tsai Ing-wen ordering the military and national security units of the country to beef up surveillance, defense, and early warning systems. This was also in response to nine Chinese warplanes reportedly flying over the air defense zone of Taiwan, further heightening tensions. Aside from its own preparations, Taiwan is also looking at how international powers, particularly the United States, will respond to Ukraine's battle versus Russia, because this could be an indication of how things will play out in case China does, in the future, decide to launch its own military operation against the island nation.

CHAPTER 5
THE ROLE OF MEDIA AND PROPAGANDA

There have been various faraway disasters, crises, and conflicts that have played out on the worldwide stage and on social media platforms over the last couple of decades, but the current escalation between Russia and Ukraine comes at a particular point in time when the use of social media apps and video sharing platforms have permeated almost every aspect of modern life. With the war in Ukraine being followed by a global audience glued to their smartphones and laptops, the various images coming out of the conflict zone are reaching corners of the globe unlike any other medium in history.

Traditional news networks and cable channels are still covering the situation in eastern Europe, but their importance in the hierarchy of information dissemination has been diminished significantly. During previous notable events such as the September 11th, 2001 terror attacks, the succeeding wars in Afghanistan and Iraq, the Arab Spring revolutions, and other manmade and natural disasters and catastrophes, the average audience would immediately turn on the television and tune in to CNN, BBC, and other major news networks.

This has changed as the rise of Facebook, Twitter, YouTube, Instagram, and TikTok rapidly skewed the viewing preferences and information consumption habits of modern society. Now, breaking news updates first spread on social media, gaining traction quickly via shares, retweets, and discussions. Streaming and other digital video content have made it possible for the average person today to keep abreast of the important events around the world without having to tune in to the cable news channels.

Even on both sides of the conflict, it has now become commonplace for either Ukrainian or Russian officials to release their statements via social media, especially Ukraine's Zelenskyy who has heavily used videos of himself in Kyiv to rally the citizens and convince the world to support their cause. Both the Russian and Ukrainian governments are using social media to disseminate information and, in the case of Russia, speed up the proliferation of propaganda and disinformation in order to control the narrative, particularly to its citizens.

Pro-Russia propaganda accounts on social media are not new, by any means. The tension between Ukraine and Russia over the separatist regions of Donetsk were fuelled largely by online destabilization and propaganda campaigns of pro-Russia accounts. Russia has been employing this online warfare strategy for many years, even before the 2014 events. In fact, at that time, General Philip Breedlove, the Supreme Allied Commander for NATO in Europe, already sounded the alarm regarding Russia's online activities, describing their communication strategy in Ukraine as "the most amazing information warfare blitzkrieg we have ever seen in the history of information warfare."

Ukraine has fought back on social media as well, attempting to push against the overwhelming flood of misinformation and inflammatory posts from the Russian online machinery. As the Russian invaders began to enter Ukraine's borders, the official Twitter account of the government of Ukraine transformed into an essential component of its strategic communication strategy. The account publishes regular new updates, patriotic content showcasing historic Ukrainian people and events, content that is critical of Russia, and even some humorous posts. These days, a large number of Ukrainians depend on Zelenskyy's Twitter account to get the quickest and most reliable information regarding the ongoing conflict, as well as the status of negotiations with other world leaders.

Ukrainian citizens are also using social media apps to document the war, detailing what is going on right in their neighborhoods, and providing the whole world with fascinating and often heartbreaking photos and videos of the ongoing conflict. But experts have also cautioned that the picture being painted on social media may not always be an accurate representation of what is really happening on the ground. War is a complicated situation regardless of the location or time in history, and social media, with its amplification of simpler, shorter, ready-for-consumption stories that often only last a few seconds, may not always be able to show the whole scene.

Jeffrey Lewis, a professor of arms control from the Middlebury Institute of International Studies, says, "You could see a TikTok video showing ten destroyed Russian tanks, but ten tanks is only a small sample of what the Russians have. It's a lot more complicated than just looking at your phone."

Social media users also have to be careful of the proliferation of fake news and disinformation regarding the events in Ukraine. In mid-March, for instance, a deepfake video that appeared to show Ukraine's President Zelenskyy ordering his troops to surrender went viral on social media. The heavily manipulated video was widely discredited, but not before making the rounds on Facebook, Twitter, Instagram, and other platforms.

Still, despite the potential problems surrounding social media use in times of war, the positive side cannot be ignored. All around Ukraine, citizens are using their online accounts to share photos and videos to the world, highlighting the atrocities being committed by Russian forces, rallying the world to come to

Ukraine's aid, and encouraging fellow Ukrainians to rise up and fight the invaders.

There have also been sweeping changes within the biggest social networking platforms themselves in response to the developments around the conflict. For instance, a Facebook post encouraging violent action against Russian troops would have been grounds for suspension in Ukraine just a couple of months ago, but now the platform allows it in the context of the ongoing war. On the other hand, the Russian state media groups that used to spread disinformation widely on Facebook have now been blocked all over Europe.

Other companies are following suit. Google has stopped showing advertising in Russia and has actively taken down YouTube videos that either misrepresent or trivialize the events happening in Ukraine. Twitter, on the other hand, now bars tweets that link directly to Russian state-sponsored media, while TikTok has blocked all video uploads from Russia, citing the fake news law that was released recently.

What the Ukraine war has also emphasized is how the social media companies should be prepared to handle events of this magnitude and act on a case-by-case basis. Katie Harbath, CEO of Anchor Change, a tech policy consultation firm, said, "The companies are building precedent as they go along. Part of my concern is that we're all thinking about the short term."

Emerson T. Brooking, a senior resident fellow from the Digital Forensic Research Lab at the Atlantic Council, adds that it is no longer feasible for social media companies to have a one-size-fits-all approach to content moderation in times of war, noting that many of them already have rules in place for elections, pandemics, and terror attacks, but not wartime.

Anchor Change's Harbath agrees, but concedes that it is a big challenge. "This is easier said than done, but I'd like to see them building out the capacity for more long-term thinking. The world keeps careening from crisis to crisis."

Where social media has been finding its way around the Ukraine crisis, traditional news media outlets have found themselves in familiar territory. Whether on air, in print, or online, covering war is something that established news outlets have already done extensively in the past, and as such, they have proven once again their mettle and importance in such times of crises.

According to Regina Lawrence, associate dean of the School of Journalism and Communication at the University of Oregon, stresses that one can see striking differences in the coverage of the current war compared to other recent US-led conflicts in the Middle East because of the differences in government rules about media access.

"In the Gulf war, the United States was leading the military charge, and that meant reporters were closely managed," Lawrence, who is also research director at the Agora Journalism Center, pointed out. Reporters were given information every day from military officials, and their access to the battlefields was limited. They were embedded with troops and weren't allowed to gather news on their own."

This has not been the case in the current Russia-Ukraine conflict, as journalists have had more freedom to cover the events on the ground. "The US government has no say in how journalists cover this, and that means there's a certain kind of openness that has been created."

On the side of Russian media, however, the exact opposite has been the situation throughout this conflict. Putin and the Russian law making assembly have signed the "fake news" law, which has been used to harass and threaten journalists and news outlets. Media practitioners have been threatened with jail time if they release news reports that are counter to the Kremlin's version of the events in Ukraine.

Officially, Russia labels its actions against Ukraine as a "peacekeeping mission" to protect the Russian-leaning separatist republics in the eastern regions that have declared themselves to be aligned with Moscow. As such, this state-owned television, radio, and print channels all parrot this narrative, and any dissenting opinions or voices are immediately silenced by authorities.

According to Andrew DeVigal, director of Agora Journalism Center, students and media observers should sit up and really monitor how the Russian disinformation machinery is attempting to control the narrative and influence the perception of people favorably toward Putin and his cohorts. "Pay attention to the disinformation that is happening with the state-run media in Russia and how it's affecting the reactions of not only non-Russians, but Russians as well," DeVigal said.

In stark contrast to how Putin has used social media and Russian media to spread wrong information, Ukraine's Zelenskyy has been cleverly using social media to rally the world to Ukraine's side and call for support. Much of his media savvy may be coming from his years of experience as an entertainer as well as his background as a lawyer. Zelenskyy was able to blend his skills in these two fields of expertise in order to lead Ukrainians through the difficult situation and also inform the world of what was happening in his country.

Kelli Matthews, a professor of social media classes in the School of Journalism and Communication at the University of Oregon, says Zelenskyy's use of social media has transformed him from a comedian, to a politician, and now a hero figure in the eyes of much of the world. "Zelenskyy is a master of using social media platforms to his country's advantage," Matthews said. Also, this image of him as a hero in this conflict "creates a rallying point for people who stand with Ukraine," according to Zelenskyy.

But it all comes back to what Putin's next move will be, and what his endgame truly is when it comes to Ukraine. Both mainstream and social media is still trying to make sense of what Putin really wants to achieve with everything that he has been doing in Ukraine so far. In an interview with *Vanity Fair,* author Peter Pomerantsev wants people following the conflict between the two countries to remember that eventually, Putin may actually be targeting something bigger, well beyond Ukraine: he might be gunning for America.

"I think we're sort of framing this as a plucky country slaying a dictatorship. But Putin is this mad stalker trying to get revenge. It's all about undermining 1989 and what he feels was an unfair defeat of the Soviet Union. He hates Ukraine because they chose a different path, and that's a challenge to the kleptocratic model he's set up. But his aim is America," according to Pomerantsev. "Listen to what the Russian propaganda is saying. It's all about you guys."

When asked how long he expects the Ukraine war to dominate the news cycle, Pomerantsev said that it will probably drag on for quite some time, and the Putin saga will continue to dominate much of the headlines for as long as he is around. "His aim is: America leaves Eastern Europe, America abandons NATO. That's the aim. He wants revenge and the undoing of the victory of democracy over dictatorship. You might want to get sick of Mr. Putin very soon, but I'm afraid you'll have to put up with him for as long as he's alive—and as far as he can go," he said.

CHAPTER 6
THE IMPACT

It is difficult to pinpoint exactly what the long-term effects of the current war between Russia and Ukraine will be, not only in the eastern European region but also globally. At the moment, the situation is still very fluid, and new developments are taking place each day that change the trajectory of the conflict. But even a few weeks into the Russian invasion of Ukrainian territory, there were already economic upheavals with worldwide repercussions already observable.

Most of the biggest economies of the world have limited trade partnerships with Russia. For instance, only 0.5 percent of the total trade of the United States comes from Russia. Trade with Russia accounts for only 2.4 percent of the Chinese economy. Because of this, one lead economist from Oxford Economics, Adam Slater, postulated that as far as any decrease in the total economic production or GDP of the world, the predicted drop will only be around 0.2 percent for 2022.

Perhaps the more far-reaching effect of the conflict, however, will be in the supplies of oil, natural gas, and metals. Russia is a major supplier of these important commodities, and because of the current situation in Ukraine, the supply chain for these commodities could be prone to disruptions as well as price volatility, and this will inevitably create a domino effect globally.

A few weeks into the crisis, the United States and other Western nations already applied pressure to Putin using strong economic sanctions on Russia. As of April 2022, the United States announced a ban on new investments in Russia, strict sanctions on two Russian-owned banks, Alfa Bank and Sberbank, and measures against large Russian-owned enterprises, Russian officials, and family members. Even the children of Putin and the extended family members of Russian Foreign Minister Sergei Lavrov were not spared.

The United Kingdom also announced sanctions on Sberbank, which is the largest Russian-owned financial institution. The United Kingdom also pledged to cease all imports of coal and oil from Russia by the end of the year. London is banning private jets chartered by Russian citizens, and has moved to sanction Wagner Group, a Russian private military firm that is believed to be a major component of the Russian armed forces.

Also, the United Kingdom will slap a 35 percent tax on certain imported products from Russia, including vodka, in a move to discourage people from patronizing them. The export of luxury goods to Russia has also been banned by the country.; the ban includes high-end fashion products, art, and luxury vehicles.

The European Union, for its part, has announced a prohibition of the export of dual-use goods to Russia. These are products that can serve both civilian and military use, including various vehicle parts. Aside from the European Union, the United States and the United Kingdom have imposed a similar ban on these dual-use items. Europe's largest bloc has also imposed heavy sanctions on over a thousand Russian citizens and businesses, including ultra-wealthy oligarchs who are closely allied with Putin.

Another significant sanction imposed by the United States, United Kingdom, European Union, and Canada was against

Russian flights. All Russian flights were banned from the airspace of these four places by early March. Prior to the blanket ban, several airlines had already announced they had suspended all flight activity over Russian airspace. This included companies such as United Airlines, American Airlines, Delta Air Lines, and United Parcel Service.

The effect of this move would be the disruption of much of the world's supply chains. For instance, the bans affect air transport between the European continent and important destinations in Asia such as South Korea, Japan, and China. The ban covers flights over Siberia, and airlines that move about 20 percent of the total air cargo of the world were immediately affected.

Because of the closed airspace, major airline companies such as Lufthansa, Air France KLM, Virgin Atlantic, and Finnair cancelled cargo flights to North Asian destinations. Meanwhile, Scandinavian carrier SAS announced that its Copenhagen-Shanghai service running once a week would be rerouted in order to avoid restricted Russian airspace, and that its Copenhagen-Tokyo flights would be stopped temporarily.

Perhaps the most significant, immediate effect of the war in Ukraine all across the world was in the oil and gas market. When Russia began its invasion of Ukraine in late February, restrictions on oil and gas imports were immediately announced by the United States, United Kingdom, and the European Union. In response, Putin threatened to stop supplying gas to countries that did not want to pay for gas imports in the ruble currency.

Then, the United States went further and announced a total ban on all oil, gas, and coal imports from Russia, while the United Kingdom started a gradual phaseout of Russian oil until the end of 2022. The European Union, meanwhile, lowered its imports of Russian gas by two-thirds, further putting the squeeze on Russia. All of these moves, as well as the general anxiety and volatility in the markets regarding the supply disruption and how long the conflict will last, have caused oil and gas prices to spike since the start of the war in Ukraine.

Russia is the world's third largest oil producer after the United States and Saudi Arabia, although only three percent of the oil that Russia produces ends up in the United States. More than half of the oil from Russia goes to the European continent, and comprises eight percent of the oil demand in the United Kingdom. With the current situation, the major economies are looking for alternative suppliers for their oil and gas needs. US President Biden announced that oil from strategic reserves will be used to offset rising fuel prices.

Another alternative option that has been explored has been increased oil production from OPEC. This oil cartel, which includes Saudi Arabia, is the source of about 60 percent of internationally traded crude oil, and thus has a crucial role in the oil price market. The United States and other Western countries have been requesting OPEC member-countries to increase their oil production in order to drive down fuel prices worldwide, but so far, none of the OPEC members have agreed to this.

Meanwhile, as major Western economies announced measures against Russian oil and gas imports, pressure mounted for the biggest multinational energy companies to stop trading with them. Among the first to pull out their Russian investment was BP, which had owned a major stake in the Russian-owned energy firm Rosneft. Shell, Equinor, and ExxonMobil have also announced that they were cutting off their Russian investments in response to the attack on Ukraine.

Financial sanctions against Russia have also been far-reaching. A number of Western countries have moved to freeze the assets of the central bank of Russia, effectively stopping it from being able to use its foreign currency reserves which stand at $630 billion. This measure caused the ruble to decrease in value by 22 percent, and caused a 14 percent increase in Russia's inflation rate and a significant increase in the cost of imported goods into the country.

Another major blow to Russia's financial system was the removal of a number of Russian financial institutions from the SWIFT messaging system. The SWIFT system acts as a worldwide financial artery that facilitates the fast transfer of money across different countries. SWIFT, or the Society for Worldwide Interbank Financial Telecommunication, is based in Belgium and connects 11,000 banks and financial providers in more than 200 nations, with an estimated 40 million messages sent daily and trillions of dollars worth of transactions.

According to the United States, United Kingdom, and European Union, shutting out Russian banks from the SWIFT system would "ensure that these banks are disconnected from the international financial system and harm their ability to operate globally," and this is intended to cripple Putin's ability to finance its operations in Ukraine. Without access to SWIFT, Russian financial institutions will have to deal directly, causing delays and additional costs, and leading to drastically reduced revenues and access for the Russian government.

In addition to the expulsion from SWIFT, the United States has now also banned Russia from accessing the $600 million it has in several US banks in order to make debt payments for its international loans. This means the Russian government would have to find another source to continue its debt repayments, or otherwise face high interest payments or worse, defaulting on the loans.

The United Kingdom has shut out the majority of Russian banks from the country's financial system, and frozen the assets of all Russian-owned banks. Also, all Russian state and big companies are currently not allowed to raise capital or get loans in the United Kingdom, while Russian citizens are limited as to how much money they can keep at British banks.

Russian citizens will also feel the pressure even further as the biggest payment processing companies—Visa, Mastercard, American Express, and Paypal—have all stopped their operations in Russia. Although Russian citizens who use Visa or Mastercard will still be able to use their cards within Russia, these cards will not work abroad, and any foreign-issued cards will not work within Russian territory.

Social media was abuzz a few weeks into the crisis in Ukraine when several major international companies announced that they were pulling out their business operations in Russia due to the conflict. Fast food giant McDonald's, for instance, announced the temporary shut down of almost 850 locations around Russia, caving in to pressure from the general public as well as shareholders who did not want the company to continue generating profits from Russia.

Coffee giant Starbucks shut down its 100 stores in Russia, while Coca-Cola, Heineken, and British American Tobacco announced the immediate cessation of their investments and operations all across the country. Meanwhile, Pepsi stopped the production and sale of its products and other brands, but said it will continue to offer some essential items. This was also the decision made by Unilever, Procter & Gamble, Nestle, and Mondelez.

Aside from food and beverage firms, other retail brands have also suspended the Russian segment of their businesses. This includes L'Oreal, Estee Lauder, Burberry, Chanel, H&M, Levi's, and Zara. Other big retail names such as Ikea, Uniqlo, and Boohoo are expected to follow suit. All around Russia, locations of these international brands and retailers have been closed due to the Ukraine conflict. Even Apple stores have suspended operations.

In the entertainment industry, there have been measures taken in protest of Putin's actions as well. Netflix has suspended its streaming service in Russia, and all future projects in the country have been put on hold for now. Major movie studios Warner Brothers, Disney, and Sony have suspended all new film releases in Russia, and Disney also stopped its TV channels from airing in the country. Meanwhile, Spotify has ceased offering its music subscription service within Russia, although the ad-supported free version still works. The three major record companies—Sony, Universal, and Warner—all closed their Russian offices.

Fallout has also taken place in the political and diplomatic scene. As the conflict raged on and images of atrocities against civilians in Ukraine began to emerge, Germany expelled 40 Russian diplomats from its territory. According to German foreign minister Annalena Baerbock, the expulsion was in response to "unbelievable brutality on the part of the Russian leadership and those who follow its propaganda."

France sent home 35 Russian diplomats, while Lithuania ordered the Russian ambassador to leave. All in all, over 250 Russian diplomats and embassy personnel have been expelled from nine countries in the European Union, as well as the United States. Reacting to the expulsions, former Russian president Dmitri Medvedev said Russia is already eyeing various counteractions. "It will be symmetrical and destructive for bilateral relations," he said.

Already, Russia has announced an export ban on over 200 of its locally-manufactured products until the end of the year. Affected exports include medical supplies, telecoms equipment, vehicle parts, agricultural products, timber, and electrical machinery. Russia has also suspended interest payments to foreign investors holding government bonds, banned Russian companies from paying their overseas shareholders, and prevented the sale of billions of dollars worth of Russian stocks and bonds by foreign investors.

With all of the back-and-forth and the aftermath of the continuing escalation of the crisis, Europe is the region of the world that seems to be at most risk economically, primarily because of the continent's dependence on energy supplies from Russia. Already, the price of natural gas in Europe has gone up by 20 percent ever since the invasion began, and is six times more than the average at the beginning of 2021. As the higher gas prices affect inflation, average Europeans have also had to shell out more for their heating expenses.

The crisis comes at a time when much of the world was hoping to bounce back economically after reeling from the COVID-19 pandemic. In Europe, however, the optimism for an economic recovery has been replaced with a generally pessimistic outlook as households struggle with higher prices and less spending money. Industries that are poised to suffer direct impact include fertilizer production, which has to be decreased because of the higher cost of natural gas. With all of these negative developments, experts warn Germany may be facing an economic recession in the first quarter of 2022.

It remains to be seen what other lingering effects the Ukraine crisis will have on the global economy. What is certain, is that for at least the next few months, or as long as the situation continues to worsen, any hopes of economic recovery from the pandemic have been shattered as the Russia-Ukraine war puts a further strain on the economic balance of the world's economies. This is why many world leaders are calling on both sides, and all parties involved directly or indirectly, to exercise caution, restraint, and try to find a diplomatic solution to the crisis as soon as possible.

CHAPTER 7

THE CURRENT SITUATION

More than the economic impact of the ongoing conflict between Russia and Ukraine, the human devastation and the refugee crisis are even more difficult to fathom. This is especially true for younger generations who are experiencing their first conflict of this scale. Fighter jets, missile attacks, devastated city centers and neighborhoods, and fleeing throngs of residents are all familiar movie scenes to the young generation, but to actually see these images playing out in real life seems surreal in 2022.

The evidence of atrocities and war crimes in different parts of Ukraine that have been perpetrated by Russian troops have pushed world leaders to increase their pressure and sanctions against Putin. In fact, in one of the strongest responses from the United Nations so far, the Russian delegation to the UN Human Rights Council was suspended on April 7th, 2022. This move came after the brutal killing of Ukrainian civilians in Bucha, a suburb of Kyiv, came to light via photos and videos.

The United States initiated a resolution to suspend Russia from the Human Rights Council, and it was brought before the UN General Assembly's 193 members, of whom 93 voted in favor of the suspension of Russia. Twenty-four voted in opposition to the resolution, while 58 abstained. This was only the second time that a country has been suspended from the council. The first time it occurred was back in 2011, when Libya was removed.

After Russia's suspension, the foreign minister of Ukraine thanked the UN for standing with his country and protesting the atrocious violations and human rights abuses of the Russian forces. "War criminals have no place in UN bodies aimed at protecting human rights. Grateful to all member states which supported the relevant UNGA resolution and chose the right side of history," Foreign Minister Dmytro Kuleba posted on Twitter.

Countries around the world have been stepping up measures against Russia as more and more reports of torture, rape, and killings of both civilians and soldiers have been verified in Ukraine. More promises of arms, equipment, and humanitarian aid have poured in, especially from the United States, with Secretary of State Antony Blinken vowing that Washington will not let up in continuing to support Ukraine with more weapons to help with its fight against Russia.

Europe is also firming up its support for Zelenskyy and the people of Ukraine, with European Commission President Ursula von der Leyen personally making a scheduled visit to Kyiv on April 8th, 2022 as a show of the bloc's unconditional support of Ukraine and condemnation of Russia. Speaking to the press in Stockholm, she said, "The Ukrainian people deserve our solidarity... I want to send a very strong message of unwavering support to the Ukrainian people and their brave fight for our common values."

Figures regarding the death toll in the various areas of fighting around Ukraine continue to change day-to-day, and verifications have become increasingly difficult. Initial estimates in the city of Mariupol in southeastern Ukraine, one area that has been continuously attacked by Russian forces and separatists for many weeks, puts the civilian death toll at around 5,000. This figure comes from pro-Russian authorities who have overtaken Mariupol, including newly-installed town mayor Konstantin Ivashchenko who said up to "60-70 percent of the housing stock has been destroyed or partially destroyed" in the city.

Meanwhile, according to official statistics released by the Office of the UN High Commissioner for Human Rights (OHCHR), as of April 5th, 2022, there have been 3,675 civilian casualties in Ukraine. Of this number, 1,480 were killed, while 2,195 were injured. Among the civilian casualties, most were a direct result of explosive weapons that were used with a wide impact range, such as shelling from heavy artillery and multiple launch rocket arms, as well as air strikes and missile attacks.

OHCHR warns, however, that the civilian casualty toll may be much higher than has been reported because of the constraints in receiving information from some areas where fighting has been significantly more intense. The regions of Donetsk (including the cities of Mariupol and Volnovakha), Kharkiv (specifically Izium), Luhansk (including Popasna) and Kyiv are of utmost concern, and authorities say civilian casualties in these regions could be much higher than reported.

Apart from the sobering statistics on casualties, the numbers regarding the worsening refugee crisis are overwhelming, to say the least. According to the UN High Commission for Refugees (UNHCR), within the first five weeks of the war, up to four million refugees fled from Ukraine and crossed the borders into surrounding countries, while millions more have been internally displaced and are still in need of aid and rescue.

As of April 6th, 2022, there are upwards of 2.5 million refugees currently in Poland, while Hungary is housing more than 662,000 more. Hungary and Moldova currently have around 400,000 Ukrainian refugees, while Slovakia has a little more than 300,000. Meanwhile, there are also around 350,000 refugees within the Russian Federation, and a little more than 18,000 currently staying in Belarus.

Speaking to CNN, UNICEF spokesperson James Elder described how dire the situation has become in Ukraine, especially for the young. "It's mind-boggling. Since the start of the war a month ago, out of every boy and girl in the country, one out of two now has had to flee their homes."

For Ukrainians who are still in the country either because they have nowhere else to go or they would rather not leave, supplies of even the most basic needs have become dangerously low, and the country's supply system has broken down. In the areas of Kharkiv and Sumy, as much as 70% of the population are now depending entirely on aid, as estimated by Steve Gordon, the humanitarian response adviser for Mercy Corps in Ukraine.

Meanwhile, Ukraine's Foreign Ministry spokesperson Oleg Nikolenko says the city of Kherson in southern Ukraine has almost completely run out of food and medicines, and this situation is becoming more common in many other Ukrainian cities and towns. As Russian forces move through the country of Ukraine, it will become more difficult for residents to procure even the most basic supplies, and humanitarian lifelines bringing essentials may be disrupted as well, thus adding to the gravity of the problem.

Worldwide, the effects on food insecurity are also being felt. With fuel prices rising, the supply of fertilizer has decreased, and this has caused a big spike in the cost of wheat, corn, soybean, and vegetable oils. Both rich and poor countries are feeling the pinch; in France, for instance, which is a developed country, the government is mulling over distributing food vouchers for low and middle income families hardest hit by the higher food prices.

French President Emmanuel Macron has described the situation as a "worldwide food crisis" exacerbated by the surge in global wheat prices. With wheat supplies suddenly unavailable from Russia and Ukraine, both of which combine to export 30% of the global wheat supply, countries heavily dependent on wheat as a food staple are facing shortages.

Even in the United States, the biggest economy in the world, the rise in food prices has impacted households. In February 2022, average food prices in the United States increased by one percent, which is already the biggest spike since April 2020. The increase has been attributed to the jump in fuel prices from the start of 2022.

There's a lot of bad news in and around this Ukraine situation, certainly. But one bright spot that analysts and international observers have, at the very least, been optimistic about is the seemingly neutral stance that China has taken. As one of the biggest economic and military powers in the world, and a close friend of Russia, many have been worried that if China actively takes the side of Putin, a larger, more global conflict could erupt, sending the situation spiralling out of control.

At least for now, China seems unwilling to ruffle feathers on either side, and instead has adopted a stance that allows it to continue its close relationship with the Russian Federation without being viewed as an outright enemy by NATO and the Western allies. The delicate balance seems to be holding, albeit precariously for now.

But where could this all end? What analysts and world leaders are hoping for is a withdrawal of Russian troops from Ukraine and an immediate end to the bloodshed, although most agree that this is as close as it can get to a miracle. In fact, most observers concede that despite Ukraine's gallant efforts to take a stand against the sustained offensive of Russia, it will only be a matter of time before Putin's forces wear down and eventually overwhelm Zelenskyy and his brave troops.

Putin is intent on installing a new regime in Kyiv that is sympathetic to Moscow, and he will do whatever he can to stop the advance of NATO in the region and prevent Ukraine from becoming an official ally of the West. According to Eurasia Group, a think-tank firm with expertise in the region, Russia will likely gain control of Eastern Ukraine at least up to the Dnipro River within the next three months, and Kyiv will likely fall after several more months, thus allowing a puppet government to be installed.

Cliff Kupchan, chairman of Eurasia Group, also predicts that a smaller, loyal Ukrainian state will possibly be headquartered in the western city of Lviv, close to the Polish border, where an exiled government will continue to lead a much-smaller Ukrainian state amidst significant support from Western allies.

In an interview with CNBC, Rand Corporation senior defense analysts Scott Boston also pointed out that Russian forces "have a whole lot of combat power left and a lot of capacity to scale up the violence, which seems to already be happening."

As to how much longer the ongoing conflict between Russia and Ukraine will last, Boston warns, "This thing could really drag on for a long time."

Can the situation be resolved? In an article they co-wrote for *Politico* magazine, two leading policymakers gave their thoughts on a way out for both sides. Alexander Dynkin, who is a Russian citizen and president of the Primakov National Research Institute of World Economy and International Affairs at the Russian Academy of Sciences, and former assistant to former Russian Prime Minister Evgeny Primakov; and Thomas Graham, a top American consultant at the Council on Foreign Relations, and senior director for Russian affairs on the National Security Council under the George W. Bush administration, gave their joint four-step plan on how the Ukraine crisis can possibly be resolved:

- Restrictions on all military activities close to the border between NATO and Russia

- Moving forward, a moratorium on eastward expansion of NATO
- Resolution of all ongoing and paused conflicts in the Balkans and former Soviet region, including Crimea, Donbas, and Kosovo
- Long-overdue modernization of the 1975 Helsinki Accords, which detailed a pan-European forum and set the principles for interstate relations between the East and West blocs.

Both Dynkin and Graham do concede that a settlement that is this comprehensive and arduous will undoubtedly require a lot of time and effort, not only between Russia and Ukraine, but also all other parties and stakeholders. However, they stress that the time to act and get this settlement started is now; otherwise, the conflict will not only drag on, but also potentially get worse.

As the two policymakers emphasized in their proposal, any diplomatic resolution that will finally bring long-lasting peace to Eastern Europe will require an understanding of how the crisis goes back not only to the 2014 revolution in Ukraine, but further back to the end of the Cold War when Russia lost many of its territories which, until now, it considers to be part of its national interests. NATO must realize that its very presence and expansion in the region threatens Putin's view of the future security and economic prosperity of Russia, and that his actions now reflect that perceived threat to his country's preeminence in the region.

If all concerned parties are truly committed to bringing about peace in this region of the world, there must be an acceptance of the fact that everyone will have to be open to significant adjustments and compromises so that larger crises can be avoided. For peace and stability to be achieved, the West must be willing to accommodate Russia's interests and satisfy minimal security stipulations without giving up any of the core principles, interests, and partnerships adhered to by the United States and its close allies. Just as it was when the Helsinki Accords were signed in 1975, in a settlement of this proportion, it is impossible for any country to get every single thing that it wants. Any final agreement will require compromises from all sides, and while this may not be the best idea, it will still be better than prolonged or intermittent armed conflicts.

AFTERWORD

As we continue to watch the events coming out of Ukraine, and try to make sense of the conflict unfolding between the two countries, the lessons of history and the realities of the collective human experience should always be our guide, shaping our perspective and bringing us to a sound, logical, and reasonable understanding of the events. Beyond the headlines, the social media posts, the shared videos and photos, and the chatter coming from different sides, armed conflicts such as the one happening at the moment in Eastern Europe give us plenty of opportunities to enhance our shared values.

Freedom, truth, and respect for the most basic human rights and liberties must always be central to society. Any attempts to undermine the pursuit of life, liberty, and happiness must be quelled and condemned, and as citizens of the world, we must be ready to stand up for what is true, actively and passionately denouncing misinformation and attempts to spread deception and division.

The saga of Russia and Ukraine will go down as among those global events that had profound and significant impacts on the course of human history. The hope is that, when our global community comes out of this dark, difficult, and tragic chapter of history, we will have learned what valuable lessons can be gleaned from what has transpired, and in the future, steps can be taken so conflicts like these will just be relics from the past. To move forward, we must sit up and take notice today, and open our eyes, hearts, and minds to the realities facing mankind.

How the whole world reacts, responds, and resolves the current showdown between Russia and Ukraine will doubtless set a precedent many years down the line. There is a grave responsibility resting squarely on the shoulders of today's leaders and citizens that will inevitably shape how democracies are protected, sovereignties are respected, and the lives of all, regardless of background or status in life, are valued in society. When all parties involved realize this immense responsibility, there will be positive and responsible changes to behaviors, actions, and considerations.

Can peace be achieved in Eastern Europe? Let us hope that, despite the seemingly insurmountable challenges lying along the path to lasting stability in the region, all sides involved will find the motivation to sit down, resolve their issues diplomatically, and work together to find a peaceful way out of this tangled, convoluted situation. Hope is not lost, but will ultimately require the unwavering commitment of all sides.

REFERENCES

Brown, B. D. (2022, February 23). *Ukraine conflict: Where are Russia's troops?* BBC News. https://www.bbc.com/news/world-europe-60158694

Conant, E. (2022, February 18). *Russia and Ukraine: the tangled history that connects—and divides—them.* National Geographic. https://www.nationalgeographic.com/history/article/russia-and-ukraine-the-tangled-history-that-connects-and-divides-them

David Goldman, CNN Business. (2022, March 24). *Gas rationing, food vouchers and hunger: Economic pain from Russia's war is getting real.* CNN. https://edition.cnn.com/2022/03/24/economy/economy-russia-ukraine-war/index.html

Dene, M., Lablow, H., & Silber, C. (2022). *Middle East Responses to the Ukraine Crisis.* The Washington Institute. https://www.washingtoninstitute.org/policy-analysis/middle-east-responses-ukraine-crisis

Fitzpatrick, S. (2022, March 3). *Ukraine as a 'borderland': a brief history of Ukraine's place between Europe and Russia.* The Conversation. https://theconversation.com/ukraine-as-a-borderland-a-brief-history-of-ukraines-place-between-europe-and-russia-178168

Green, T. (2022, March 1). *Russia's invasion of Ukraine has already changed the world as we know it.* NPR.Org. https://choice.npr.org/index.html?origin=https://www.npr.org/2022/03/01/1083686062/russias-invasion-of-ukrainian-has-already-changed-the-world-as-we-know-it

Harding, L. (2022, March 6). *Ukraine can win, says US, as fightback frustrates Putin's plan for swift victory.* The Guardian. https://www.theguardian.com/world/2022/mar/05/ukraine-claims-battlefield-successes-as-mariupol-evacuation-falls-apart-russia

History.com Editors. (2020, February 28). *Russian Revolution.* HISTORY. https://www.history.com/topics/russia/russian-revolution

History.com Editors. (2022, February 23). *Soviet Union.* HISTORY. https://www.history.com/topics/russia/history-of-the-soviet-union#:%7Ehttps://www.history.com/topics/russia/history-of-the-soviet-union#:%7E:text=The%20Soviet%20Union%20had%20its,and%20bloody%20civil%20war%20followed.:text=The%20Soviet%20Union%20had%20its,and%20bloody%20civil%20war%20followed.

Ivanova, P., & Olearchyk, R. (2022, February 6). *Ukraine and Russia: how have relations soured since the fall of the Soviet Union?* Financial Times. https://www.ft.com/content/0a44d4a1-b8b2-4c9d-b07b-63b029c9d6bb

Jewers, Chris & Pleasance, Chris. (2022, April 14) MailOnline https://www.dailymail.co.uk/news/article-10720215/Russias-Black-Sea-flagship-Moskva-SUNK-Moscows-defence-agency-admits.html

Jordans, F. (2022, February 22). *Ukraine-Russia: Germany suspends Nord Stream 2 gas pipeline.* AP NEWS. https://apnews.com/article/russia-ukraine-business-germany-europe-berlin-79e3dafb0d231f6a033613b7dab78cdf

Kagan, F. W., Barros, G., & Stepanenko, K. (2022). *RUSSIAN OFFENSIVE CAMPAIGN ASSESSMENT, MARCH 4.* Institute For The Study of War. https://understandingwar.org/backgrounder/russian-offensive-campaign-assessment-march-4

Lawmakers give Putin permission to use force outside Russia. (2022, February 22). POLITICO. https://www.politico.-

com / news / 2022 / 02 / 22 / putin-permission-force-outside-russia-00010637

Mirovalev, M. (2019, February 22). *Ukraine at crossroads five years after 'revolution of dignity.'* News | Al Jazeera. https:// www.al-jazeera.com / news / 2019 / 2 / 22 / ukraine-at-crossroads-five-years-after-revolution-of-dignity

Pifer, S., & Thoburn, H. (2016, July 29). *Ukraine: Protests and Memories of the Orange Revolution.* Brookings. https:// www.brookings.edu / blog / up-front / 2013 / 11 / 26 / ukraine-protests-and-memories-of-the-orange-revolution /

Pompeo, J. (2022, March 4). *Sizing Up Media Coverage of Russia's Attack on Ukraine.* Vanity Fair. https:// www.vanityfair.-com / news / 2022 / 03 / sizing-up-media-coverage-of-russias-attack-on-ukraine

Radcliffe, D. (2022, March 14). *SOJC experts weigh in on media coverage of Ukraine war.* Around the O. https:// around.uore-gon.edu / content / sojc-experts-weigh-media-coverage-ukraine-war

Reals, T., & Sundby, A. (2022, March 23). *Russia's war in Ukraine: How it came to this.* CBS News. https:// www.cbsnews.-com / news / ukraine-news-russia-war-how-we-got-here /

Roy, D. (2022, March 25). *How Bad Is Ukraine's Humanitarian Crisis?* Council on Foreign Relations. https:// www.cfr.org / in-brief / ukraine-humanitarian-crisis-refugees-aid

Shepardson, D., Freed, J., & Chee, F. Y. (2022, March 2). *U.S. follows Canada, Europe on Russian aircraft ban.* Reuters. https:// www.reuters.com / business / airspace-closures-after-ukraine-invasion-stretch-global-supply-chains-2022-03-01 /

Sonne, P., Dixon, R., & Stern, D. L. (2021, October 30). *Russian troop movements near Ukraine border prompt concern in U.S., Europe.* Washington Post. https:// www.washingtonpost.-

com/world/russian-troop-movements-near-ukraine-border-prompt-concern-in-us-europe/2021/10/30/c122e57c-3983-11ec-9662-399cfa75efee_story.html

Talmazan, Y. (2022, February 25). *How Ukraine's president Volodymyr Zelenskyy transformed from entertainer to fatigue-clad leader.* NBC News. https://www.nbcnews.com/news/world/zelenskyy-ukraine-russia-putin-invasion-rcna17661

The Economist. (2022, February 16). *What did Ukraine's revolution in 2014 achieve?* https://www.economist.com/the-economist-explains/2022/02/16/what-did-ukraines-revolution-in-2014-achieve

Ukraine - The crisis in Crimea and eastern Ukraine. (n.d.). Encyclopedia Britannica. https://www.britannica.com/place/Ukraine/The-crisis-in-Crimea-and-eastern-Ukraine

United Nations Human Rights Office of the High Commissioner. (2022). *Ukraine: civilian casualty update 5 April 2022.* United Nations. https://www.ohchr.org/en/news/2022/04/ukraine-civilian-casualty-update-5-april-2022

VOA Learning English. (2022, March 6). *The Worldwide Effects of Russia's Invasion of Ukraine.* VOA. https://learningenglish.voanews.com/a/the-worldwide-effects-of-russia-s-invasion-of-ukraine/6468531.html

CPSIA information can be obtained
at www.ICGtesting.com
Printed in the USA
BVHW031516230622
640504BV00013B/235